PRAISE FOR *THE HOPE RAISERS*

"Suthar's gift for inspirational storytelling and the courageous visionaries he meets in Korogocho should raise hope in all of us."—**Tim Crothers, author of** *The Queen of Katwe*

"*The Hope Raisers* is a deeply uplifting story that needs to be told. Daniel, Mutura, and Lucy's journeys demonstrate first-hand the magnitude of the impact we can create by working together, strengthening the solidarities among global citizens in the quest for humanity of the planet."—**Willy Mutunga, chief justice and president of the Supreme Court, Republic of Kenya, 2011–2016**

"An undeniably compelling story of the incredible power of young people. Nihar Suthar's book not only celebrates the Hope Raisers, a group of young Kenyans transforming their community, but also inspires all of us who seek to make an impact and contribute to progress in our communities. A must-read book."—**Raphael Obonyo, public policy analyst and expert with the United Nations**

"This story portrays the real-life struggles of so many and is an exact representation of the mood of most days in this part of Africa. It's left me motivated to do everything I can to create change and assist in empowering those who need help. This story truly is a deep representation of this side of life."—**Mercy Masika, award-winning songwriter and United Nations High Commissioner for Refugees Goodwill Ambassador**

THE HOPE RAISERS

THE HOPE RAISERS

*How a Group of Young Kenyans Fought to
Transform Their Slum and Inspire a Community*

NIHAR SUTHAR

ROWMAN & LITTLEFIELD
Lanham • Boulder • New York • London

Published by Rowman & Littlefield
An imprint of The Rowman & Littlefield Publishing Group, Inc.
4501 Forbes Boulevard, Suite 200, Lanham, Maryland 20706
www.rowman.com

86-90 Paul Street, London EC2A 4NE, United Kingdom

British Library Cataloguing in Publication Information Available

Library of Congress Cataloging-in-Publication Data Available

ISBN 978-1-5381-6873-8 (cloth) |
ISBN 978-1-5381-6874-5 (epub)

*To my guru Mahant Swami Maharaj,
who taught me that changing the world
starts with simply believing you can.*

Contents

Acknowledgments   xi
A Glimpse into Korogocho   xiii

CHAPTER 1: Life in the Dump   1
CHAPTER 2: Dogs on the Street   19
CHAPTER 3: Birth of the Hope Raisers   33
CHAPTER 4: The G8 Summit   41
CHAPTER 5: A Failed Upgrading Program   49
CHAPTER 6: An Unexpected Road   59
CHAPTER 7: Fat Women Can Skate Too   69
CHAPTER 8: Emergence of a Skating Team   77
CHAPTER 9: A Difficult Debut   85
CHAPTER 10: Unsustainable Success   97
CHAPTER 11: Aspirations beyond Skating   105
CHAPTER 12: Passport to South Africa   119
CHAPTER 13: Nyali Beach   125
CHAPTER 14: Adventures across the World   135

Epilogue: The Hope Raisers Live On   159
Guide to Korogocho   163
For Book Clubs and Classrooms   167
Help Raise More Hope in Korogocho   169
Notes   171
Bibliography   173
Index   177
About the Author   179

Acknowledgments

One of the first questions I'm asked when I speak to anyone about the Hope Raisers is, "How did you discover their story?"

In 2017, I was lucky enough to stumble upon a short article about the skating team in *Quartz Africa* written by Ariel Zirulnick. I owe her a deep thank-you for both intriguing me and inspiring me to learn more.

Soon thereafter, I was able to connect with Daniel Onyango and Mutura Kuria over the phone, who invited me to visit Korogocho. I took them up on the offer and knew a day after arriving that the story of the Hope Raisers was much deeper than just an article. I needed to write a book.

Since then, I've had the fortune of returning to Korogocho numerous times. During each trip, Daniel and Mutura have spent countless hours coordinating logistics, organizing interviews, and sharing intricate details of their own experiences. Writing this book would not have been possible without their help.

I also can't thank Lucy Achieng, Chumbana Omari, Jackline Auma, Mama Bonie, Kelvin Owino, and Charles Chege enough for their time participating in interviews and warm hospitality. I'll never forget it.

Throughout the entirety of this project, I was lucky to be surrounded by a phenomenal team that believed in its impact. I'd like to express my appreciation to my agent, Anne Devlin;

my editor, Richard Lynch; and the entire team at Rowman & Littlefield for helping me bring this book to life with utmost quality.

Finally, I owe a great deal of gratitude to my own family and close friends for their never-ending support and sacrifices during the four years I was intensely concentrated on writing and traveling to Kenya, whether mentally or physically.

A Glimpse into Korogocho

Korogocho was all I knew. I had no idea that life was different outside the slum. I assumed that the rest of the world was as dark as Korogocho.

—Mutura Kuria

Everything used to be so bad in Korogocho. People murdered each other. Kids took knives when they went to school. You could not even walk on the streets without getting mugged. I thank God for somehow allowing me to raise five kids here. There were times I thought we would not make it. Many days I did not even have enough money to buy food for my kids. Thank God we survived.

—Mama Bonie (Mutura's mother)

My dad works as a factory laborer in the industrial area of Nairobi. He walks 9 kilometers [5.6 miles] between Korogocho and his job in Nairobi every day. It takes him two hours one way. He is one of the lucky ones who is employed.

—Daniel Onyango

A lot of girls here engage in prostitution. If they need money but can't find a way to get it, then they go to gangsters who can give it to them. They give their bodies to the guys who have good money.

—LUCY ACHIENG

Rent in Korogocho is very expensive. I think people here are good-hearted, but because they cannot afford things like rent, they become thieves. I see them steal purses and rip necklaces from people's necks all the time.

—CHUMBANA OMARI

When I first came to Korogocho in 1993, I had no job. There was no security either. Once, thieves came into my house and stole everything I owned. Living here was so difficult that I would desperately pray I made it through each day.

—JACKLINE AUMA (CHUMBANA'S MOTHER)

CHAPTER ONE

Life in the Dump

Trash pickers dig through heaps of garbage at the Dandora dumpsite, hoping to find enough food for their families or recyclables they can resell.
COURTESY OF KATHARINA ELLEKE

A YELLOW DUMP TRUCK BUMPED TOWARD THE EAST OF NAI-robi, leaving billowing clouds of dust in its wake. Below the windshield, a black grille prominently displayed "Auman," the name of the truck's Chinese manufacturer. Ironically, the proud name hung on a vehicle that was nothing to brag about. One of the headlights was shattered. The solid metal bumper was somehow mangled, giving off a presence of having emerged from war. Raw waste piled high in the truck bed oozed, leaving ugly brown streaks flowing down the side panels. Three Kenyan men, dressed in tar-ridden jeans and torn collared shirts, sat on top of the mound like kings. They wore cheap cotton hats to combat the sharp wind that pierced through them. The intensity of the slight chill in the air increased as the truck merged onto a highway and picked up speed.

The three men had made this trip thousands of times before. Every morning, they followed the same routine, waking up at 3:00 a.m. to collect trash from one of Nairobi's neighborhoods and transport it to the Dandora dumpsite. Dandora was the only landfill for the 3.5 million residents of Nairobi. With an area of 30 acres, it was one of the largest dumpsites in the world.

Even though they came daily, they never got used to the dump's overwhelming expanse. Trash was stacked in towers so high that the entire dump truck could disappear without anyone noticing or caring. More than 850 tons of waste from Nairobi made its way to Dandora every day. Officially full since 2001, it still remained in operation. Fires raged in every corner as operatives burned what they could in a desperate effort to create more space.

The driver followed a path back to a familiar area where the garbage reached the height of a three-story building. Used syringes and glass pieces crunched under the tires, popping like firecrackers, left in the wake of gruesome drug and sex crimes by gangs fighting each other over possession of attractive women. Six gangs controlled the Dandora dumpsite: Weighing Bridge, Gaza, Portmore, 41, Kajiji, and Ngenge.

All truck operators were required to pay them dumping fees. The entitlement resulted in turf wars, often involving gunfire as one group attempted to overpower another for a larger share of the profits. To limit deadly altercations from breaking out, gang leaders negotiated pacts between each other, granting them exclusive rights to collect fees for assigned territories on particular days. Those who interfered suffered consequences.

This day was the Gaza gang's turn to profit. Gaza was formed by fifteen boys with nothing left to live on. Out of desperation, they turned to lives of crime. Members bragged about their crimes, without any fear of the police or authorities. During robberies, they attacked their victims by stabbing or shooting them, whether it was necessary or not.

Tiger, a senior Gaza member, led the crude operation. The truck driver cranked down his window and pressed some bills into Tiger's outstretched hand. Tiger inspected the contents of the vehicle and then motioned to where the driver should unload the trash. Dozens of dumpsite scavengers caused a commotion, screaming in Swahili, the national language of Kenya.

One woman's voice resonated over the uproar. "We have not looked there yet, *hatukuangalia hapo bado!*" She didn't want new waste to cover what was still left to explore.

Tiger shot an irritated look at her then turned his back, as if she was unworthy of his attention. In an unusual gesture of compassion, he redirected the driver of the truck to another area of the dumpsite.

"Thank you, *asante sana*," she said with a sigh of relief.

Tiger was not oblivious to what life was like being a trash picker. He had scavenged through trash piles for scraps of food himself. On his luckiest days, he would find either *chombo*— leftovers discarded from in-flight meals that wealthy travelers did not care to eat—or *anyona*—fancy bread thrown out because it was too old to serve in high-end bakeries.

Trash pickers paid 200 shillings (USD 2) each morning to Gaza for the "privilege" to dig through the heaps of trash. They prayed they might be rewarded with good fortune for what, to them, was a hefty price. Stumbling upon some *chombo* or *anyona* released the pressure of having to feed themselves and their families.

Women who toiled as trash pickers avoided eye contact with anybody. They just wanted to do what was necessary to survive without causing trouble or being harassed. Gang members whistled and smacked the butts of attractive women they wanted as girlfriends. These women had to tolerate the advances if they wanted to continue picking trash at Dandora. The controlling gangs had the power to do whatever they pleased.

As important as avoiding run-ins with gang members, female trash pickers did not want to advertise that they worked at the dumpsite to survive. They felt more worthless than the garbage around them, forced to depend on the unwanted junk of others to live. The women fed their children such unsavory food that even ravenous vultures left it behind.

The raptors hovered above the pickers in flocks, circling patiently until they sensed an appealing meal. Their large jet-black wings cast shadows in the rays of the sun below. When they spotted an enticing treasure, they swooped in and claimed it without hesitation. These vultures often claimed the best tidbits of food before trash pickers could.

Pickers took breaks to forget about what they were being forced to do. They sat on top of garbage towers, flipping through torn-up magazines or books. The colorful illustrations made them feel a bit better.

Despite the circumstances, one of the trash pickers always did her best to stay positive. Her smile revealed her slightly chipped teeth and her warm, caring nature. She was known as Mama Bonie by the locals. She got the name when she took over the task of raising her grandson whose name was Bonie. Her daughter gave birth to him at a very young age and moved nine hours away to the eastern coast of Kenya for a job after finishing school, where she could not afford to take him. Mama Bonie took over full-time responsibility of caring for him, even though she relied on trash picking to support her four other children.

At five o'clock each morning, she arrived to search through junk with a group of her friends. Trash picking was a special bond that glued them together, and working alone at the dump-site was ill advised. Gang members preyed on anybody who looked like an easy target, especially children, women, or the elderly, even though there was little worth stealing from these people because they were already so poor. The only belongings that remained for women to give were their own bodies, which they sometimes offered for sex out of desperation.

To avoid unwanted attention, Mama Bonie dressed modestly. She wore an old T-shirt with a faded skirt that stretched down to her ankles. On her head, she wore a dark red *kitamba*, or headdress, wrapped around and around like a turban. She was older and slightly chubby, so the male gangsters did not ogle at her like they did with the slender young women. On some days, Mama Bonie wished she was more noticeable to the gangsters. Girlfriends of gang members got exclusive access to all the best areas of the dumpsite, and she could use that advantage to support her family.

Mama Bonie relied on finding old paper, plastic, or glass that she could sell to recyclers. She made 10 shillings (USD 0.10) per kilogram of paper or plastic and 25 shillings (USD 0.25) per kilogram of glass. She could earn even more for metals, though finding any was rare. It was 75 shillings (USD 0.75) per kilogram of aluminum and 300 shillings (USD 3) per kilogram of copper. Finding any of the more valuable items became increasingly difficult because there were more trash pickers than ever before.

Most pickers did not realize how hazardous the dumpsite was. The odors were repulsive and burned in people's nostrils. Novice trash pickers sometimes fainted because they were not accustomed to the strength of the smells. The trash incineration generated suffocating smoke and fumes that caused coughing, breathing, and eye problems and likely led to cancer.

Trash pickers were too poor to afford shoes, so if they were not careful, they could also step on smoldering fragments of trash and burn themselves severely. Pickers referred to these spots as "boilers." They were so hazardous that even Kenyans who knew nothing about trash picking heard the horror stories about them. Mama Bonie witnessed encounters with boilers on multiple occasions. She saw more than one child leaving Dandora sobbing, with bubbly blisters from the burns on their bodies. The blisters left behind scars as permanent reminders of the brutal conditions at the dumpsite. There was little she could do to help. She was no doctor. She might find an old rag to wrap around their burns. Most were left to suffer with no one's care.

Mama Bonie could not neglect herself to help others. If she failed to collect enough paper, plastic, or glass for the day, her own family would go hungry. Her primary purpose was to stay at the dumpsite until she found enough of value that she could sell it and provide for her family.

Mama Bonie looked toward the area where the driver of the yellow truck dumped his trash, wondering if there was anything worthwhile.

Faint smoke rose up around it. One of her friends yelled, "Watch out for a boiler here, *chunga boiler hapa!*" to alert the others.

Mama Bonie acknowledged the warning. Her experience gave her the courage to get closer to boilers than most other trash pickers. Because few people dared to approach the boilers, she could sometimes find more valuable scraps there. She plodded her way through the mounds of trash in the direction of the boiler.

In her rush to meet her quota for the day and get out of the awful dump, Mama Bonie trod over an unstable heap of trash with charred remains, mud, and loose rocks. Suddenly, she found herself skidding down the mound with an avalanche of garbage and rocks following her. She tried to regain control, but she lost her balance and threw her hands out to brace for the fall. Her hands absorbed most of the impact as she landed, and a sharp, stinging sensation shot from her palm all the way down her spine. Mama Bonie closed her eyes and knew better than to be so clumsy.

At first, she thought the stinging was from the force of her weight on her hand, but it lingered after the fall. She opened her eyes and saw splotches of blood covering the trash around her. Startled, she turned over the palm of her hand and was met with part of an old soda bottle poking out from the base of her thumb. She got lightheaded at the sight.

"Help me, *nisaidie!*" she called out to anybody who could hear her.

Three of her friends appeared by her side.

"Oh my God, *mungu wangu,*" one of them gasped.

Another friend grasped her bloody hand and said, "Do not worry, everything will be fine. *Usijali, kila kitu itakuwa sawa.*" She ripped the glass out of her palm.

The pain pierced Mama Bonie again as the glass was forced out. In an instant, the sensation disappeared, and the deep gash filled with a stream of blood. One of the friends gave her a handkerchief. She did not question where it came from or how clean it was; she just wrapped it around her hand to cover the gash. The thin cloth quickly soaked with blood.

"It looks very bad, *umekatwa sana*. Do you want to go to the clinic?" offered one of her friends. "We can take you."

Mama Bonie declined. "No, no. It's okay, *ni sawa*."

She knew that she should go, but going to the clinic was often more trouble than it was worth. There were few public health clinics in the area, and they were almost always jammed with endless lines of patients. The small staff of two or three people—a nurse, lab tech, and sometimes a clinical assistant—did their best to offer comprehensive care with the limited supplies they had. Her injury was much less severe compared to the patients suffering from childbirth complications, HIV, or AIDS. She did not want to take away from the help they desperately needed for a hand that she could treat herself.

"We are leaving soon anyways," Mama Bonie said. The group of friends usually left Dandora around 8:00 a.m. It only took them a few hours because they had limited access.

Continuing to apply steady pressure with the thin hand-kerchief on her hand, Mama Bonie winced in pain. She noticed she could not move her thumb like normal and thought the glass had injured a nerve or muscle in her hand. She did not tell her friends for fear of worrying them. She could not afford to take any time off, and she still had more to do that day.

A voice inside her head comforted her, thinking that it would not be the worst thing in the world if she could never return. She disliked the dumpsite and knew she was poisoning herself each time she came. Recently, officials from the United Nations Environment Programme had measured harmful chemicals like lead, mercury, and cadmium there at the highest levels ever. Experts recommend that lead and cadmium levels should never exceed 150 and 5 parts per million, respectively. Near Dandora, these levels were more than 13,500 and 1,058 parts per million, respectively.[1] The contamination created a difficult dilemma. On one hand, the dumpsite posed a serious health hazard to trash pickers and the two hundred thousand people who lived nearby. On the other hand, it was often their only source of income.

Mama Bonie threw the dark canvas sack that contained her findings for the day over her shoulder. Everyone else used a similar sack. Together, they navigated out of the sprawling site. Near the outskirts of the dump a handful of kids chased each other, blissfully unaffected by the overpowering stenches and toxic runoff. They squealed in delight as they took turns kicking a worn-out ball between them.

A young girl called out, "Mama Bonie! What happened to you?" Her name was Lucy Achieng, an orphan whose mother and father had passed away a few years earlier. The people left to take care of her were her stepfather and stepbrother, but her stepfather was never around, and her stepbrother was deeply involved in one of the gangs. He would bring back different girls every night to sleep with.

Having been around the gangs and the prostitution scene at the dumpsite, these girls were very aggressive. They abused Lucy verbally and physically, often for no reason. She was easy to take advantage of due to her quiet nature and young age. Lucy realized they wanted to feel like they were in power by treating somebody else like they were treated for all of their lives. It was a demoralizing environment to be trapped in. To escape, she came to the outskirts of Dandora and was there playing soccer every morning when Mama Bonie left the site.

"I just had a little accident, Lucy," Mama Bonie explained. "You pay attention, or you could get hurt too. It's dangerous here."

"Don't worry about me. I am unstoppable. I'm going to become the top soccer player in all of Kenya," Lucy dreamed aloud. She was determined to break free from the path of prostitution and early marriage that she saw the girls her step-brother brought back from the dumpsite choose.

On the outskirts of a dumpsite where thousands of people felt more worthless than the trash they picked, dozens of kids like Lucy were the happiest they had ever been in their lives. Their dreams had no limits. Mama Bonie hoped Lucy got a chance to achieve her vision.

As Mama Bonie and her friends headed on toward town, her throbbing thumb reminded her of her predicament. A sinking feeling told her that the injury was more serious than she originally thought. After working at the dumpsite for a year, it felt like every time she started to gain some momentum, something catastrophic came along to halt her progress. The last nine years of her life were littered with misfortune.

Mama Bonie's small hometown, Githunguri, was about an hour north of Nairobi. It was an agricultural community, known for its expanse of farms and dairy cows. Most residents lived in modest, rural houses and immersed themselves in farming. Back then, Mama Bonie's life was perfect. She was happily married with kids, and her financial situation was stable. To make extra money, she bought milk from the local farmers and helped them distribute it to wealthier customers in Nairobi.

Her world began to flip upside down as she started having frequent arguments with her husband. They became progressively more serious, and it wore them both down. Finally, the marriage ended in divorce.

Mama Bonie left with her five children and continued supporting them with her milk business. It went well for a few years. In 1997, a dispute in Kenya's presidential election destroyed even that because of unrest.

Daniel arap Moi, acting president since 1978, decided to run for a fifth term. Fourteen other candidates planned to stand up against him, determined to end his reign. Everybody assumed Moi would win another term because of the large field of opponents. Each would only divert a small percentage of the votes. Top political experts predicted that Moi would take more than 40 percent and win by a good margin.

The weeks leading up to Kenyan elections are always tense due to fear of corruption and tribal conflicts. Kenya's population of fifty-five million is split into forty-two different ethnic groups, so there are many opportunities for issues to arise as each tribe supports its own candidate. Skirmishes occur but usually remain minor.

Moi intentionally exploited the tribal tensions to his advantage. He made smaller tribes fear domination by the larger ones. His tactics further divided the groups, and, like a volcano showing signs of activity, the tensions were ready to explode.

When the vote took place, terrible weather, logistical problems, and disorganization led to low turnout. The presidential contenders accused the Kenyan Electoral Commission of rigging the election, declaring that the commission sent too few ballots to their strongholds to inhibit voting. Moi charged the commission with manipulating the election in favor of the opposition.

Tribes erupted, taking out their frustrations on each other through vicious attacks. More than one hundred thousand Kenyans abandoned their homes to escape the brutality. In retaliation and protest of the system, some groups destroyed voter cards and burned ballot boxes.

Due to the violence, Mama Bonie's customers fled for their safety. Having to support five children, she looked for any other work that she could find. She heard of a clothing factory near Dandora whose owner desperately needed staff, so she took her kids, an old mattress, and some clothes and boarded a bus to Nairobi. There, she hitched a ride with a truck driver going to Dandora. It was quite a risk, but luckily, she found the factory and convinced the owner to give her work sewing clothes. She toiled for long hours in atrocious conditions and it was a depressing job, but what mattered was that it gave her enough to survive and to support her children.

Her ears permanently rang from the loud noises, and she coughed constantly from the harmful fiber dust. Fortunately, she made a friend who came to the rescue. He was looking for someone to care for his pigs. While Mama Bonie did not have experience with pigs, she had grown up around many animals in Githunguri. Desperate to get out of the clothing factory, she persuaded him that she could handle the responsibility.

She taught herself how to care for the pigs. It was much better than suffering inside the factory, and she found some satisfaction in caring for the pigs like she might her own children. She fed them well with scraps from the Dandora dumpsite, following the lead of other seasoned owners.

Bad luck continued to haunt her, and the pigs caught a strain of foot-and-mouth disease. There was nothing Mama Bonie could do about it. All of them died. Assuming it was a freak occurrence, her friend invested in more pigs. Within a few months, they also caught the same disease and died. Mama Bonie's friend was unable to afford more pigs, so her job caring for the pigs ended.

Not sure what else to do, Mama Bonie continued going to the dumpsite to scrounge for scraps. Instead of searching for food to feed the pigs, she became a trash picker, searching for valuable treasures that she could sell to feed herself and her children. This became her means of sustenance, but her injury now threatened to end that too.

After Mama Bonie crossed back into Korogocho, a major slum bordering Dandora, she was surrounded by the morning bustle of fellow trash pickers organizing their findings from the dump to sell. In hopes of beating the rush at the recycling site, Mama Bonie and her friends walked past the other pickers and went directly toward the town center. Houses made of flimsy, rusted tin sheets stood on both sides of the dirt road. The sheets were left over from old housing projects or discarded by factories in Nairobi. Cardboard pieces lay on top of some of the structures to act as roofs. Every time it rained, residents needed to deal with flooding in their homes and water damage to the roofs.

Swahili hip-hop songs blasted from old radios, filling the street with sound. Mama Bonie felt the eyes of local villagers penetrating through her as sharply as the glass that had punctured her hand earlier. Luckily, she was a familiar face in this part of town, or she and her friends would not have made it past them alive. Residents regularly assaulted outsiders. The relationship between even those from different parts of Korogocho was rocky and unstable.

A distinct tribe or ethnic group was associated with each one of the nine separate villages in Korogocho. It was the fourth-largest slum settlement in Kenya, with somewhere between 150,000 and 200,000 residents. Land within Korogocho was originally set aside for a smaller population of people to fill low-income housing projects. Throughout the years, immigrants who could not be accommodated in the housing arrangements of Nairobi and people evicted from private land or other upper-class settlements were squeezed into the approximately 1-to-1.5-square-kilometer area (approximately .39 to .58 square miles).

Korogocho became associated with low status. Even Kenyan national authorities looked down on the entire slum as a criminal settlement. Feeling insignificant and neglected, residents set up independent markets without aid from the government. An impressive food industry sprouted up, and reselling items collected from the Dandora dumpsite grew exponentially.

There were two paths to get to the center of the slum where Mama Bonie and her friends could sell their dumpsite findings. The first was Grogon Road, rumored to be the most dangerous road in all of Korogocho. It went directly through Grogon, the village where most of the gangs that controlled the Dandora dumpsite were based. They randomly attacked anybody who dared to enter. Their leaders orchestrated all the activities at Dandora from afar and stayed nestled away within the village like royalty. Events at the dump were reported to them by their comrades. Everybody, including top politicians in Kenya, knew not to disturb the gang leaders or else get on their bad side. Even the police feared intervening.

The second path was Main Road. It went around most of the more dangerous areas of Grogon. While it was a safer option, the road connected with the end of Grogon Road. Many people took Main Road in hopes of bypassing Grogon entirely, but gang members lurked at the intersection. Travelers who were not alert could find themselves snatched and dragged down Grogon Road by the gangsters, where the gangsters then did whatever they pleased. Once somebody got dragged down Grogon Road, the best scenario they could hope for was to make it out alive. Mama Bonie and her friends always took Main Road, avoiding the risky areas as much as possible. Being in a large group also made them poor targets.

Main Road was an endless line of shanty structures that residents converted into storefronts. Faded signs indicated everything they were selling. Everything from homemade food to jewelry, clothes, and electronics were there, most of the items likely recovered from the dumpsite.

Mama Bonie smiled at the sellers and greeted them as she passed by. Thick smoke drifted out of one of the shops as the owner prepared a dish of rice, beans, cabbage, and fresh chapatis, or flatbread, for a child. The smell of the chapatis reminded Mama Bonie how hungry she was. When she got her money from the recycler, she would go back home and make something to eat.

The pleasant aroma of the chapatis got drowned out by raw sewage. Even in Korogocho, there was a small site where locals threw their trash before it made its way to Dandora. The slum lacked a sewage system, so runoff got mixed with the waste, creating a smelly sludge. The stench was an indicator as to how close she was to the recycling center, because the worst of the smell came from close to there.

Upon arrival, she saw many trash pickers already lined up outside to sell their finds. This time of day was the most hectic. Most pickers went to Dandora early in the morning to find the best items from the previous night. They ended up meeting at the recycling center by about 10:00 a.m. Two workers sat outside chatting with each other in Swahili. They were in charge of inspecting, weighing, and paying trash pickers for the items they brought to sell.

The workers did not recycle anything in Korogocho. They lacked the equipment to do so. Like all the other buildings, the recycling center was made of sheets of rusted, flimsy tin that could cave in at any time. Instead of being a serious recycling operation, the building just functioned as a collection center. Once materials were gathered in bulk, the workers hauled the junk to big recycling facilities outside Korogocho.

When Mama Bonie reached the front of the line, she dumped the contents of her sack on the ground without interrupting their dialogue. Recyclers took inspections more seriously these days, as trash pickers were mixing rocks and other random objects with their findings lately to increase weight and payment. The workers glanced through Mama Bonie's items to make sure there were no nonrecyclables. Once satisfied, they had her place the contents on the scale. Mama Bonie first put all the paper back into the sack so she could weigh them together. She took her time, ensuring that everything was properly separated and so she got paid what she deserved.

"Bitch, *mbwa jike*! Hurry up, everybody else is waiting in line! We don't have all day!" one of the workers yelled suddenly.

Mama Bonie rushed to put the rest of the paper products into her sack. She then hooked it onto the old scale. "These are all paper items," she said.

The man waited for the needle to settle. "You have seven kilograms of paper here," he said. That was worth 70 shillings (USD 0.70). Mama Bonie depended on the more expensive materials, like glass, to contribute most to her profits.

As he tossed her paper recyclables off to a pile on the side, she rushed to sort the rest of her plastic and glass items on the ground before he could call her something vulgar again. She did not like being called names. Unfortunately, it was common in Korogocho.

"Do you have anything else to recycle or are you done?" the man asked, hoping to shoo Mama Bonie away.

"I still have more to sell," she replied.

He shook his head in annoyance and returned to his conversation with the other worker. He was more engrossed in his chat than the other things Mama Bonie had to sell. She finished putting the plastic in the sack and hooked it on the scale. While doing that, she felt a sharp sting in her palm. Under the handkerchief, blood was still seeping from the base of her thumb.

"These are plastics," said Mama Bonie.

The man glanced at the reading. He was uninterested in her injury. "There is nine kilograms of plastic here," he said.

Mama Bonie looked at the scale to read it herself. She double-checked because the scale was prone to errors. The recyclers did not care about its accuracy. Any underestimate meant they paid less for whatever they were purchasing. In fact, some trash pickers claimed some recyclers tampered with the scales or added counterweights to make weight read in their favor.

The needle was barely visible due to the scratches and stains covering the glass. It did not help her assessments that she was unfamiliar with using scales. It seemed that the needle was close enough to nine kilograms.

The man removed the sack and hurled the contents toward a pile of plastics. Mama Bonie placed the glass inside the sack and onto the scale. She did not have as much as usual today. The reading on the scale would determine if she could feed her family tonight.

"You have four kilograms of glass," said the worker.

Mama Bonie sighed in relief and smiled, knowing that she would have enough money for today.

The man reached into his pocket and pulled out a faded pouch where he kept money. He counted 260 shillings (USD 2.60) as payment for Mama Bonie's items. The bills were waterlogged and torn from living through the harsh conditions of Korogocho. Money that came into town virtually remained forever as it got redistributed within the slum.

Mama Bonie snatched up the money like an addict. "Thank you, *asante sana!*" she said, and immediately tucked the bills out of sight in the pocket of her skirt. Flashing even a small amount of money near the recycling center could make her an easy target for criminals. They sometimes loitered in the area, knowing it was busy with trash pickers. She kept quiet while waiting for her friends to finish selling their items.

Once they all received their money, the women began the journey back home. Many of them worked doing odd jobs around Korogocho and would for the rest of the day. Others just returned home and waited until the next day to go back to the dumpsite. Knowing she made enough money for the day, Mama Bonie decided to nurse her hand back to health instead of working more.

CHAPTER TWO

Dogs on the Street

Mama Bonie pictured near Dandora, where she worked as one of often thousands of trash pickers to survive. COURTESY OF JOHN MACHARIA

Mama Bonie breathed a heavy sigh of relief as Ngomongo came into sight. Ngomongo was where she lived and one of the most unstable villages in all of Korogocho. People from the Luo ethnic group who inhabited the area had developed an intense hatred toward the government. In the past, government officials drove the Luos from Nairobi by stoning them. As a result, they became protective of their territory and were hostile toward anyone who entered, especially those who seemed to have a connection to the government.

Despite the reputation of Ngomongo, Mama Bonie always felt happy to be home after a long morning at the dump. She would have some time to relax and forget about her thumb and the dumpsite for the time being.

As she got closer to her house, she noticed her son Mutura—a short, dark-skinned boy—sitting on the ground sobbing. Normally he was waiting in the house. Her time for relaxing would have to wait.

She called out to him and broke into a sprint, fearing he was sick or had been robbed or attacked by one of the gangs. Mutura lifted his head, like a crane struggling to hoist a heavy load. He stared at his mother with his face soaked from a stream of tears.

Mama Bonie wrapped him up in the safety of her arms like a lioness protecting her cub from danger. She wiped the tears from his face, careful not to use her wounded hand.

"What's wrong?" Mama Bonie asked, searching him for injuries.

"We got kicked out of our house," Mutura managed to croak in between sobs.

"Who threw you out?! What did they say? Are you hurt?" Mama Bonie questioned.

Mutura put his head down, still shaking from the incident. "I'm not sure; it was some man," he said. "I was sleeping when he came. He kicked in the door and woke me up and told me

we owed money. He dragged me outside and locked me out."
He pointed to a rusted padlock hanging from the tin door
behind them. "He said we do not deserve to live here. He said
that we have to live like dogs on the street until we pay."

Mama Bonie drew Mutura closer into her arms. "Don't
worry, we won't have to live anywhere on the street. It will be
okay."

"Do we owe money to that man? I'm scared," said Mutura.

Mama Bonie hated questions where answers couldn't
shield her children from the burden of adult problems.

"Yes, we do owe money to that man. He is our landlord.
I told him that I would pay but I have not yet," Mama Bonie
explained.

Her relationship with the landlord was fragile. Occasionally, she felt like they were on the best of terms. Other times,
he threatened to throw them out of their house. She thought
this tumultuous behavior was her landlord's personality, but
she found out that her friends had similar problems and that
relationships with landlords around Korogocho were tricky to
manage in general.

Throughout time, this situation became worse. Tenants
accused their landlords of being corrupt. In many cases, landlords were close friends to Kenya's national politicians or were
politicians themselves. It was no surprise that nothing was
done to improve the situation. The landlords continued to
increase their riches at the expense of the poor residents who
remained in their shanty structures.

"How much do we owe?" Mutura tugged at his mother's
T-shirt.

Mama Bonie hesitated to respond. She knew her son too
well. If she told him about a problem, he felt obligated to help.
She remembered one week where she did not make enough
money to be able to buy food for her children. Mutura wanted
to help, so she sent him to the village chief because she heard

that the chief sometimes provided food to residents in dire need. A village chief is the appointed leader of a community, similar to mayors or other elected political officials. Mutura came back devastated and empty handed. The family had to survive for nearly a week with just the few morsels they could scrape together.

"We owe about 3,000 shillings," she confessed. Mutura went dead silent, trying to comprehend the value of such a large figure. It was 30 U.S. dollars. Mama Bonie only had 60 shillings (USD 0.60) for food, or else she could not pay to work at the dumpsite the next day. It felt like a pretty hopeless situation to owe 3,000 shillings. Most people in Korogocho would be lucky to accumulate a savings of that amount over their lifetimes.

"I will work and help get the money we owe," said Mutura. This was the reaction Mama Bonie expected. His desire to help was an admirable quality, but she preferred that he focus on school.

"Your studies are more important," she replied. She had enrolled Mutura in a high school about three hours outside of Korogocho, and it was arduous to get him to that point. Previously, he dropped out of school after getting involved with a gang. They passed the time with mischievous activities. Many of them eventually graduated up to more serious crime. After two years, members from St. John's Community Church inspired him to return to school.

Mutura left off at grade six but used his charm to sweet-talk his way into grade eight. Upon returning, he felt a renewed sense of motivation. He studied so hard for the admittance exam for high school that he got the highest score out of all his classmates. Mama Bonie was unpleasantly surprised when she found out how much tuition fees would be in high school. They could not afford it.

Because he loved learning, Mutura decided to join grade eight a second time until they could afford the tuition for high school. He again outscored all his classmates on the final exam. After seeing his performance, members of St. John's rallied together and sponsored him for high school. Few kids got such an opportunity, which was why his mother did not want him to throw it away.

In the past, she had been able to convince the landlord to grant an extension on their debt. She prayed that he would show mercy again.

"Wait here and watch our things," she said. "I am going to find the landlord to talk to him."

Mama Bonie knew that he was probably still going from house to house, terrorizing tenants. She asked a neighbor, who was washing her clothes in a green plastic bucket full of murky water, if she knew where he went. She pointed toward Highridge Road.

Mama Bonie hustled off to Highridge. It was one of the nine villages in Korogocho known for its Somali population. Residents migrated there from Somalia and northeastern parts of Kenya where Islam was the predominant religion. Women covered their heads with loose hijabs, or head coverings, to maintain their modesty and privacy. They built a small mosque to congregate for daily prayers.

She spotted her landlord accompanied by a very strong man. His muscles bulged under his tattered shirt, and he had an uninviting scowl plastered on his face.

Approaching her landlord, Mama Bonie asked, "Hello, *jambo*! Can I talk to you?"

The man in the tattered shirt burst out laughing.

"Excuse my vigilante here, Grace," answered the landlord. "He is passionate about enforcing the law with useless tenants who fail to pay their rent on time."

Mama Bonie was surprised to hear him call her Grace. Everybody had referred to her as Mama Bonie for so long that her real name seemed foreign.

"So, what are you doing here?" he continued. "Do you have my money?"

"I just need to talk to you." Mama Bonie started searching for a way to appeal to his emotions.

The muscled thug laughed. "I hope you both have lots of fun," he said, then winked and walked away.

The landlord assessed her from top to bottom. "Let's go inside so we have some privacy," he suggested, pointing to a small, rusted structure near them. The small house belonged to one of his tenants.

"We can just speak here," Mama Bonie countered.

"Full privacy is better. Let's go in," he pressed.

Mama Bonie did not budge. She just shook her head.

Attacks, rapes, and muggings were common in Korogocho. The village chief said there were more than fifteen reported cases per day. She herself once got ambushed by gangsters on the bridge crossing from Lucky Summer, one of the wealthier estates neighboring Korogocho, to Ngomongo. They appeared from both ends and trapped her in the middle, leaving her with no escape. The gangsters attacked her and stole the money she earned that day. When they left, Mama Bonie fell to a heap on the ground and sobbed against the cold, jagged metal of the bridge for hours. She felt lucky that the gangsters did not stab her and throw her into the dirty river waters below. At times, they even raped their victims. She owed money to a lot of people, and they would have no sympathy about her being attacked. Throwing herself into the waters below might bring her peace.

The thought of her children saved her. She returned home to them and cried throughout the entire night. Her life would not get any easier, but she learned an important lesson. In

Korogocho, she needed to stay alert when out in public by herself. Women were susceptible to being targeted. Since that incident, she only hung around people she trusted with her life. Her landlord was not one of them. He preyed on the less fortunate and might do anything in a setting where nobody was watching.

"Tenants here have no respect for their landlords!" he said.

"I have respect for you. You have always been very understanding and accommodating to me and my family. Without you, we would not have a place to stay," acknowledged Mama Bonie softly.

The landlord knew when his tenants were buttering him up. "What do you want?" he asked.

"You locked my house earlier today," she responded.

The landlord smirked, cutting her off before she could go any further. "Do you know why? I don't like worthless tenants who do not pay their rent."

"Yes, I owe you more than 3,000 shillings," Mama Bonie admitted, hoping to make him satisfied by recognizing his power.

"Thirty-two hundred shillings to be exact," he stated. "You owe me four full months' rent. I should be charging you extra fees for paying late!"

Mama Bonie continued to flatter him. "I know, most other landlords would charge a fee. But I know that you are compassionate and understanding. You have made Korogocho a better place. I feel lucky that you are my landlord." She could see cracks starting to appear in his facade. "Me and my children want to continue living in this place if you will allow us to. I owe you so much more than this. I have 30 shillings I can give you right now toward my payment." With that, she pulled out a few wrinkled bills.

The landlord groaned in disgust. "Just stop. If you want to live on my property, you need to give me real money."

"I have 10 more shillings," begged Mama Bonie, pulling out more money. She desperately hoped it would satisfy him. It would leave her with only 20 more shillings (USD 0.20), which she needed for food. "This is all that I have. I will be able to pay the rest back soon."

"Everybody tells me that they will pay me back soon. I'm not running a charity," he snarled.

"I know you are not. I will pay back what I owe, and even more." Mama Bonie spoke with confidence.

That got the landlord's attention. He was too greedy to reject it. "How much more will you give me?"

Mama Bonie knew she could not afford anything extra. "I will give you an additional 500 shillings," she blurted out anyway. She would figure out how to come by it later. For now, she just needed the accommodation to stay with her children.

"Okay. If you don't get me 500 shillings by next month, I can guarantee that I will kick you out," he threatened.

Their conversation was interrupted. "You both are already finished?! That was fast work!" squealed the landlord's vigilante. Mama Bonie cringed at his voice.

"We're done. Grace just knew exactly what I wanted." The landlord laughed. "Her structure is locked. Go down to Ngomongo and unlock it for her," he instructed.

"Oh, she put you in that much of a good mood?" The vigilante looked surprised. "Grace, let's go to Ngomongo together. I can also use a mood boost on the way." He looked as if he might try to lead her into a back alley without anybody noticing.

"You can just meet me there with the key when you are ready." She turned and began walking away as fast as she could.

"Dog, *mbwa!*" he snorted. Mama Bonie did not bother to turn around or slow down. What mattered was that she had reached an agreement with her landlord.

She saw Mutura crouching in the dirt outside their home as she approached. A few friends from St. John's had joined him after she left. He only got the chance to catch up with them during holidays because he attended school far away. They were gathered around a plastic rice cooker, taking turns sticking their fingers inside and grabbing handfuls of some soggy food. She wondered where the rice cooker came from but was thankful for it. Mutura eating now meant she had to feed him less later.

One of the boys greeted her. "Mama Bonie! How are you, *habari yako?*"

She laughed. Daniel Onyango was one of Mutura's very good friends. They met at St. John's when they were just eleven years old. Daniel was dark skinned, tall, and extremely skinny. He wore a shirt that was at least three sizes too big for him, probably handed down through an overseas charity.

"Fine, *nzuri*. What are you eating?" Mama Bonie asked.

"Rice and beans, *wali madodo*. Would you like some?" offered Daniel, who always tried to help others.

Mama Bonie felt pangs of hunger that had stayed with her since she finished working at the dumpsite.

"Thank you, *asante sana*, but I am not hungry," she lied. "You enjoy it." She was supposed to be the one to give to the kids in Korogocho, not take from them.

Daniel continued digging in, picking out the beans from the rice. Mama Bonie stood impatiently beside her house, waiting for the landlord's vigilante to unlock the door. If he did not arrive within the next few minutes, she would try cutting the lock off herself. She only hesitated because breaking a lock while behind on rent gave the landlord legal leverage to remove tenants using force if necessary.

Before she gave in to impulse, she spotted the vigilante coming down the road. The scowl returned to his face. As he approached, he did not make eye contact or communicate with her. Mama Bonie was glad she had offended him.

He produced a ring with dozens of keys. She hoped that he knew which one to use so he would get out of her sight. On his first try, the padlock snapped open. He slipped it off and kicked the old tin door open, releasing some of his wrath toward Mama Bonie on it.

"Thank you, *asante sana*," Mama Bonie said, inviting the vigilante to leave. He just glared before stuffing the keys into his pocket and walking away. She looked up into the bright sky and thanked God for answering her desperate prayers.

"Mutura! Everything is all right now! *Kila kitu iko sawa sasa!*" Mama Bonie said to Mutura.

He jumped up with his mouth full of rice and ran to give his mother a hug. For now, at least, they could continue with their routine living in Korogocho.

They settled back into their normal pattern. He washed her dirty clothes from the dumpsite in a bucket and swept the mud floor of their small house to remove debris. When evening came around, Mama Bonie gave Mutura the 20 shillings she had left and sent him to buy food for dinner. She usually went herself but could not muster up the energy.

Having to go out to purchase food gave Mutura an excuse to spend more time with his friends. Mutura asked Daniel, who was still hanging around on the street, if he wanted to come. Daniel instantly agreed. Together, they walked to a nearby vendor they knew well.

The owner's makeshift shop on the street used an old wooden shipping pallet as a tabletop and unevenly cut pieces of wood for legs. All of it likely came from Dandora. To block the rays of sun beating down on him, he tied a cheap umbrella to the tabletop.

"Mutura, Daniel! What's up, *niaje?*" he called as he saw the boys approaching. "What would you like? I have some fresh lettuce I got delivered yesterday." He pointed proudly to leaves tied together with twine and arranged on the table. He had painted a big red number 5 on a cardboard sign, indicating that each package of lettuce leaves was 5 shillings (USD 0.05). "That looks very fresh," Mutura admitted. He knew that his mother would not approve of him buying lettuce. It would do nothing to satisfy his family's hunger. He had to make sure he used the 20 shillings (USD 0.20) to buy the most filling food he could. Mama Bonie usually purchased maize meal. It was cheap and she used it to make *ugali*—a staple food across Kenya. Kenyans boil the maize meal in water until it reaches a stiff doughlike consistency. It is usually served with chicken, fish, or vegetables.

"I will take 20 shillings of maize meal, *unga*," he said to the vendor while handing some bills to him. The seller scooped out the maize meal while Mutura held up a small, dirty canvas sack. Most people in Korogocho carried these types of sacks when they went shopping because street vendors did not have any bags to offer. The seller dumped about half a kilogram of the maize meal into his sack.

"Anything for you?" the seller asked, turning to Daniel.

Daniel shook his head. Mutura pinched the top of the sack shut and thanked the seller. The boys began to walk back in the direction of his home.

"What are you doing tomorrow?" Daniel asked Mutura. "You should come visit St. John's in the morning."

"What is happening there?" Mutura inquired.

"I forgot to tell you! I put together a band with some boys from the church recently. We're practicing tomorrow. It would be fun if you joined. I'm working on original lyrics," said Daniel.

The idea intrigued Mutura. He dabbled with the saxophone in high school but never played with a band. He agreed to join.

When Mutura got home, his mother was already setting up her stove.

"Sorry to keep you waiting." Mutura handed the sack to her.

Mama Bonie was impatient to eat. She threw some charcoal in the stove and placed the only pot she owned on top. Puffs of thick, white smoke began to fill the air, causing her to break into a coughing fit. Cooking with charcoal in such a small space was dangerous for her and her children's health, but she had no other option.

As the sun was starting to set, darkness posed another challenge. Electricity was limited in Korogocho, and all Mama Bonie had for light was a small paraffin lamp to use while she was cooking. The fire from the stove was brighter than the pathetic lamp. Luckily Mama Bonie had cooked *ugali* so many times before that she could make it blindfolded if she had to. She continued stirring it with her wooden spoon until she got it to the perfect consistency.

Once it reached a thick texture, she served it to her children in plastic bowls. The bowls were mismatched as Mama Bonie collected them from various parts of Korogocho over the years. She sat down to have the leftovers only after her children ate enough. By this point, she felt lightheaded because she had not eaten in so long.

Most Kenyans traditionally eat food with their right hands. As she tried to eat, she was overcome by unbearable pain in her hand. She felt certain that she would have to find a new job. There was no way she could work at the dumpsite without being able to pick anything up. Another injury, or something worse, might be more likely with the use of just one hand.

She decided to solve these problems tomorrow and focused on the food she felt lucky to have in front of her. The *ugali* was a bit bland, and she wished that she could have afforded some meat to eat with it. The only condiment in her house was salt. She sprinkled some on top and devoured everything in minutes.

After finishing, Mama Bonie cleaned up and moved all the kitchenware to the side to create space for her children to sleep. In Korogocho, everybody slept on the floor of their single-room houses without luxuries like mattresses. The room was only about 10x10 feet, so the kitchen functioned as the bedroom, living room, and even the bathroom. Whenever people could not make it outside in time, or if it was the middle of the night, they would relieve themselves in plastic bags, tie them, and fling them out the door. These plastic bags became known as flying toilets. Oftentimes they gathered in large piles outside homes or were seen floating down the Mathare River near Korogocho.

Mama Bonie wished her children a "good night, *lala salama*." Today they were going to bed late. Mutura looked at his mother with his eyes already drooping. She knew he would fall asleep almost instantly. Usually, they were in bed by 8:00 p.m. because there was nothing to do without electricity once it got dark.

As Mutura drifted off into a slumber, he had thoughts of being dragged outside by their landlord. He hoped something like that would never happen again. Mutura wasn't sure what he would do, or how he would do it, but he vowed to one day create change in his slum.

The next morning, Mutura awoke to see his mother sorting through a pile of clothes. He realized she did not go to the dumpsite and asked her why.

"I hurt my thumb yesterday at the dumpsite. I am going to try selling clothes for a few days," she explained.

Concern flashed across Mutura's eyes. "Why didn't you tell me you hurt your thumb? Do you need anything? I can stay home today and help you sell clothes." He had planned to go meet Daniel at St. John's, but the band would be there another day. Nothing was more important to Mutura than his mother.

"It is okay! Unless you want to become a village boy again, you should go to St. John's," Mama Bonie insisted, settling the matter.

Mutura nodded. He wanted to help, but he knew he was not going to win the argument. She was right. It was important for him to remain involved at St. John's. It had a very positive influence on him.

CHAPTER THREE

Birth of the Hope Raisers

Daniel and Mutura during a Hope Raisers band practice at St. John's Church. The Hope Raisers rehearsed inside an empty classroom with instruments they received from donors of St. John's. COURTESY OF HOPE RAISERS

ST. JOHN'S WAS A KIND OF GLUE THAT HELD KOROGOCHO together. It was the place where residents went to pray, play sports, learn music, read books, attend school, and take part in community-wide events. Before it opened, none of this was well organized. In a slum full of so much darkness, the church provided some light.

The religious center was funded by the Catholic Church. Its main mission was to identify with the struggles of living in Korogocho. The church gained the respect of the local residents due to the missionaries. They lived among the community and initiated projects to solve problems in the slum.

Whenever Mutura went to St. John's, he made time to participate in such activities involving younger kids. From tutoring to playing sports and music, he gave back by being a constructive role model. With so many kids there, he knew he would inevitably influence more than just one.

He ran into Daniel as soon as he walked through the gate to the center. Daniel introduced the three other boys—Simon, Robert, and Isaiah—as members of the band. Mutura didn't know them well but had seen them around St. John's before. He wondered what kind of music they would play but assumed they would focus on more trendy pop, hip-hop, and reggae songs.

Daniel led Mutura back to an empty classroom where they practiced. On the way, they passed students inside other classrooms. The creaky wooden picnic tables were worn down from the thousands of students who used them over the years. Mutura remembered sitting at desks like those when he was in primary school and knew how lucky the students were to even have them. At other schools across Kenya and Africa, children were not so fortunate. Many of them spread their sparse belongings out on muddy floors and used large rocks as their desks.

"I wrote some new song lyrics for today," Daniel told the group as they were busy setting up the instruments. They had a keyboard, guitar, and saxophone that they received from donors working with St. John's. The incredible milestone would improve the quality of their music. Before, they just sang a cappella. That wasn't ideal, because Daniel was the only good singer in the group. The addition of instruments allowed the other boys to try something they might be better at.

When they were ready, Daniel explained his new song. "I'll sing the lyrics for you first so you can hear what they sound like. Then, we can add the instruments." He cleared his throat and began singing.

Somebody tell me why, somebody tell me why. Somebody tell me why life is like this in the motherland Africa.

I wake up in the morning, turn on the radio, I heard the news that five young girls have been killed. The suspect was their father, leaving me to wonder, and what is wrong and why do these evil things.

Every day our brothers killing one another, we take a look of the war that was sin afoot. Even in Somalia and here in Kenya, I want an answer, can somebody tell me why?

Survival for the fittest, rule of the jungle. Contamination, that is life in Africa. Look at our structures, even our resources, all of them, in the hands of only few.

Corruption is protruding, poverty increasing, every day in the continent of Africa. Why is it in Africa, all these problems, can somebody please tell tell me why?

Somebody tell me why, somebody tell me why. Somebody tell me why life is like this in the motherland Africa.[1]

Simon spoke up. "Those are very different lyrics!" he said, not quite sure how to react.

"I think music like this can change Korogocho," Daniel said. "Pop music these days is out of touch with reality. Their lyrics only talk about rich lifestyles, sex, and drugs. Maybe that's okay for people in Nairobi and in big cities. That is not our reality here." Daniel followed the news outside Korogocho. As a result, he became convinced to explore the connection between the slums and the outside world. Music was the best way he knew how.

Mutura saw people around Korogocho crowded around the few radios that existed, singing lyrics of the newest catchy pop and hip-hop songs. They memorized songs even though they did not relate to the lyrics themselves.

"Do you think people want to listen to songs about all the problems in the slums?" challenged Robert. "Maybe they like listening to the pop songs because it makes them forget about the world they live in."

Daniel shrugged his shoulders. "I think songs like this can be really important, and we won't know unless we try." He recited a fact he heard in school. "Sixty or 70 percent of people living around Nairobi live in informal settlements like us. I really think they have to be represented somehow."

"Well, let's practice, then," Simon declared, sounding slightly unconvinced.

"I'll play the guitar," Robert called.

"I can take the keyboard," stated Isaiah.

Daniel asked Mutura what he wanted to do. Mutura knew he was not a good singer. Luckily, he was familiar with the saxophone that remained unclaimed.

Mutura never mentioned his saxophone abilities to Daniel. "I played the saxophone a few times at school," he answered, understating his skill.

"No need for me to show you anything, then," Daniel said with a laugh. "Let's go for it! I will sing. You all can accompany with the instruments." He handed the boys their parts with notes scribbled on paper.

Daniel's soothing and pleasant voice filled the room as he sang. Then the instruments joined in. The sounds of the guitar and keyboard made him cringe. He wrote the harmony, and it was obvious that the boys did not know how to read notes or play the instruments. He waited for the squeal of the saxophone to complete the chaotic mix. Surprisingly, the opposite happened. When the saxophone entered, it was smooth and melodic. Mutura played effortlessly. Daniel almost stopped midsong to ask how Mutura learned to play so well.

When the boys made it to the end of the song, Daniel lightheartedly smacked Mutura on the arm. "How have you only played a few times before?" he joked. "You sound like a professional!"

"I've been taking some saxophone lessons in high school. Maybe I'm better than I thought." Mutura laughed.

Daniel set a goal to help the rest of the boys play their instruments as well as Mutura. They practiced the song several more times together but were not much better by the end of the session. Drastic improvement would not come overnight, and Daniel tried to stay patient. The boys were just playing for fun. He knew it was not fair to push them too aggressively. He could only hope they would progress over time.

Daniel hoped Mutura would be able to be part of the band. Not only would he be a valuable player, but he might also inspire the others.

"Are you sure you have to go back to school?" Daniel half joked with him.

"I can't waste this opportunity I have for school. I have to finish," Mutura confessed. "I will return to Korogocho again in a few months during school holidays."

"We will have the saxophone waiting for you," persuaded Daniel, "so long as you promise to play it when you are back."

Mutura agreed and Daniel smiled, satisfied his band would have at least one good musician in the future.

Ready to end practice for the day, they walked outside and saw a group of boys and girls playing soccer on the basketball court beside the classrooms. The fences that enclosed the area were so tall that they made St. John's look like a prison ground. Anybody unfamiliar with the church could have likely mistaken its large gates as meant to prevent anyone inside from escaping.

The reality was that the barriers were needed for protection. Because community members congregated at St. John's, it made individuals an easy target. When Mutura was younger, there were countless instances of gang members coming to steal food. They struck right at lunchtime in plain sight. Once, gang members appeared with machetes. The kids, fearing for their lives, dropped everything and ran away. The gang snatched it all and left the kids without anything to eat that day.

"What's the news, *eh habari?* Can we join your soccer game?" Daniel asked one of the girls playing on the court.

She waved to them to join, so the band members jumped in. The girl was an intense player, weaving through all the defenders and leaving them behind as they attempted to keep up. A few times, she even whizzed by Daniel and Mutura.

"What is your name?" asked Daniel, out of breath during one of the breaks. He was impressed with her speed and athleticism.

"My name is Lucy Achieng," she answered.

Mutura realized who she was. "Do you often play soccer near Dandora? My mother mentioned you before. Her name is Mama Bonie."

Lucy smiled. "Of course! I play soccer near Dandora almost every day. It is my passion and my goal to become the best soccer player here."

Daniel and Mutura were impressed that a young girl like Lucy was dreaming so ambitiously.

"But I didn't see Mama Bonie this morning at Dandora," she added.

"My mom hurt her hand yesterday at the dumpsite so she's taking a break from there for a few days," explained Mutura.

Lucy remembered Mama Bonie acting very nonchalant about the injury. "Is she okay?" she asked.

"She hasn't told me much. She thinks I'll worry about her and get distracted from school," Mutura admitted. "But she should be fine."

Lucy was relieved. She whispered a quick prayer for Mama Bonie's recovery. Something about Mama Bonie inspired Lucy to push herself harder.

After the break, Lucy returned to the game with a renewed spirit. She continued playing soccer with the boys until they were exhausted from chasing her around the court. They enjoyed the game while they could, but smoke from Dandora began to billow onto the court, which made some start breaking out into coughing fits. It became difficult to play, and they were forced to stop.

Mutura started home happy at the end of the day, reflecting on everything he had done. Upon his arrival, however, he saw his mother sitting outside wrapping her hand with a ragged cloth. His happiness faded.

"How is your hand?" he asked.

"I just cleaned it with water," said Mama Bonie.

"Does it feel better?" Mutura asked, nodding, knowing wounds could easily get infected if not properly cared for.

"I'm still having trouble moving my thumb," Mama Bonie admitted.

"You should go to the clinic!" Mutura became more concerned.

Mama Bonie told him not to worry. She mentioned that while he was at St. John's, she had some success reselling clothes from vendors around Korogocho in richer, neighboring estates. It was a new business she could pursue while nursing her hand back to health.

Between his day at St. John's and his mother's good news about the clothes, Mutura beamed, feeling that there could be joyful days in Korogocho after all.

"I practiced playing music with Daniel and some of his friends today," Mutura excitedly told his mother. "They started a band. Daniel wrote lyrics for a new song."

"What kind of song did Daniel write?" Mama Bonie asked.

"It was a very different song about the struggles in Korogocho. He liked my playing and wanted me to be part of the band. I will practice with them again when I come back," said Mutura.

A few days later, he went back to school. Whenever he returned to Korogocho, he maintained his promise to play saxophone in Daniel's band. Each time, the members became a little bit better. Their music went from sounding very rough to more refined. It was a powerful evolution to witness. The group was playing with greater purpose and sincerity as well.

Once when Mutura came back, Daniel told him that the boys chose a name. "We are now the Hope Raisers," he said. "The goal of our music is to give hope to people in Korogocho."

Mutura loved the name and premise of the group. "It's perfect. The Hope Raisers will become known for creating change in the community." The boys were all inspired by the prospects of the future. Now, the Hope Raisers had to make it a reality.

CHAPTER FOUR

The G8 Summit

The Hope Raisers band performs their song "G8" on the streets of Korogocho. Daniel set up shows around the slum upon direction from Father Moschetti. COURTESY OF HOPE RAISERS

FOR A WHILE, DANIEL WROTE LYRICS AND KEPT THE SONGS among members of his band. Paying attention to the news, he heard about the G8 Summit. It was a summit organized as a venue to help resolve differences and encourage positive economic decisions. It brought together leaders of the richest industrialized countries like France, Germany, Italy, Japan, the United Kingdom, the United States, Canada, and Russia. The summit sparked debate, protests, and demonstrations. Because of the influence of these nations, it created opportunities for global change and the entire event got leveraged into a platform for activist pressure.

The United Kingdom was hosting the thirty-first G8 Summit on July 6–8, 2005. The government announced that one of the main focuses of the summit would be on the lack of economic development in Africa. Prior to the start of the summit, rumors swirled of planned demonstrations meant to aggressively promote this agenda. In response, the British government engaged security forces from around the world. This included more than ten thousand police officers, numerous U.S. Marines, a Special Air Service team, snipers, and countless intelligence agencies that monitored credible threats. The security forces were said to cost close to 200 million U.S. dollars in total.

The security team did its best to maintain peace, arresting more than seven hundred people and charging three hundred others connected to riots. Most of these arrests did nothing but further fuel the ferocity of later demonstrations. One protest in Edinburgh attracted more than two hundred thousand people, the largest demonstration ever in Scottish history. It was organized by Make Poverty History, an organization with the ultimate goal of eliminating global poverty. One of the appeals of the group was to drop the drowning debt owed by African nations to rich and developed countries. Overall, this accounted for more than 40 billion U.S. dollars. It was astonishing that this plea was well received at the summit. Leaders of all eight countries came to an agreement to drop the debt.

They did not drop the debt of every country but did for eighteen nations that fell within the group of heavily indebted poor countries (HIPC). Nations with that classification have the highest levels of poverty and debt, and it made them eligible for special assistance. News about the historic debt cancellation spread around the world like wildfire. Most people reacted to it with enthusiasm, but residents of African nations not included in the relief program reacted with outrage.

Kenya, for example, was a country crushed by debt, but not impoverished enough to officially fall into the HIPC group. Members of the public, media, and Kenyan government challenged that their debt should be canceled along with the eighteen other countries. They organized international campaigns in retaliation.

Living in Korogocho, Daniel knew the hardships of living in poverty firsthand. When he learned of the movement forming, he wanted the Hope Raisers to be part of it. If they could portray the real experiences of local people to help erase Kenya's debt, then the government could invest that money to create jobs and improve the quality of life in slums like Korogocho. This was a real chance to create change and bring hope to the people of Korogocho.

Daniel got an idea to record a song about their struggles. He thought the Hope Raisers could film a music video around Korogocho, showcasing the hardships that were being ignored. He became inspired and wrote the lyrics of a provocative song to promote his plea:

"G8"

G8, G8, we got a question for you, G8 G8, we got a question for you. Why do you want us to suffer? Why do you want us to perish?

Yet you know, we are the creditors. Yet you know that, we are the creditors. Cancel debts, cancel debts, you the G8. Cancel debts, cancel debts, you the G8.

Continent of Africa, a lot of suffering. Poverty and hunger, people are dying. Wars are going on, this is instilled in us. Justice in our continent, because of the debt. G8 you fail us, we really owe you, it's not true, it's not true. You are the robbers, you've stolen from us, our resources. Cancel debts, cancel debts, you the G8!

G8, G8, we got a question for you, G8 G8, we got a question for you. Why do you want us to suffer? Why do you want us to perish?

Yet you know, we are the creditors. Yet you know that, we are the creditors. Cancel debts, cancel debts, you the G8. Cancel debts, cancel debts, you the G8.

Sanctions of economy, because of the debt. Sanctions of environment, reason the debts. Lacking of employment, creating otherness. Youth are affected, drug addicted. Add the thieves yea, because of the debts. Cancel debts, cancel debts, you the G8!

G8, G8, we got a question for you, G8 G8, we got a question for you. Why do you want us to suffer? Why do you want us to perish?

Yet you know, we are the creditors. Yet you know that, we are the creditors. Cancel debts, cancel debts, you the G8. Cancel debts, cancel debts, you the G8.

You took our people, to your continent. Worked for you without pay, and thus you killed them. Funded your industry, you see my people. Now that you're rich man, with our resources. It's not right, it's not right. You have to cancel debts. All the countries. All the G8. Like Italia. Together Britain. Even United States. Cancel debts, cancel debts, you the G8!

G8, G8, we got a question for you, G8 G8, we got a question for you. Why do you want us to suffer? Why do you want us to perish?

Yet you know, we are the creditors. Yet you know that, we are the creditors. Cancel debts, cancel debts, you the G8. Cancel debts, cancel debts, you the G8.

Daniel told Simon, Robert, and Isaiah about his idea, showed them his song, and encouraged them to practice it so they could get involved in the debt cancellation movement.

Mutura returned to Korogocho a few times as the song was developing and was moved by the potential impact it could have. He helped push the band members to continue rehearsing and making it better. Practices became more frequent and intense.

Like everyone who went to St. John's, Lucy would hear the band practicing the song while she was playing soccer. She even went to watch them rehearse. At one rehearsal, Lucy asked Daniel if she could try playing an instrument. Daniel showed her a few notes on the keyboard. He was surprised when she replicated them perfectly and offered to teach her more.

Lucy did not love music enough to give up soccer, but she enjoyed trying the instruments and being around Daniel's band when they were practicing. Sometimes when they were rehearsing, the whole group playing soccer would stop their match and go listen. Slowly, more people visiting St. John's started doing the same.

Even Father Moschetti took notice of the music. He asked the boys what they were rehearsing for. He was interested in music and wanted to invite more local artists to perform at St. John's. There was a large amphitheater with cement benches, normally used for religious services and sermons, that was perfect for large performances. Unfortunately, he never found musicians in Korogocho.

Daniel told Father Moschetti about his plans to capitalize on the publicity the G8 Summit generated to help change Korogocho, explaining that was why his band was preparing. Father Moschetti was intrigued. "Tell me more about the change you want to create," he said. Father Moschetti always hoped to help solve the community's social justice issues.

"The song we are working on is about the debt cancellation campaigns," explained Daniel.

Father Moschetti took part in orchestrating some of the campaigns to deal with Kenya's debt. "How do you plan to spread awareness of your song?" he asked.

"I'm not sure," Daniel admitted, pondering over the question.

"You should perform this song in the community so people can hear it. You can organize a performance here in the amphitheater too. It will start getting attention," Father Moschetti said, fully convinced about the song's message. "I am going to be meeting some Italian government officials in Europe next month," he continued. "If you have a recording of the song, I will present it to them then." Father Moschetti was originally from Italy and quite well connected through the Catholic Church.

Although he lacked the equipment and did not know how he would record, Daniel promised that he would get Father Moschetti a recording of the song. Meanwhile he would start organizing Hope Raisers performances so they could perfect their song.

Daniel set up small shows on the streets of Korogocho and played the "G8" song with the Hope Raisers wherever they could find an audience. This led to some opportunities to perform at community events, congregations, and even festivals around Korogocho.

At one festival, the boys got a lucky break. While playing, they noticed somebody in the audience recording their song with a camcorder. Daniel did not take his eyes off the person with the camcorder throughout the entire song.

As soon as they finished, Daniel hurried into the audience, determined to track down the person with the camcorder. He located the person and got his attention. Daniel struck up a conversation with him, and they instantly made a connection.

Andrea Dal Piaz was in the area volunteering for a nongovernmental organization. He resonated so much with the Hope Raisers' mission that he offered to help record the "G8" video.

In the coming days, the band prepared for the shoot with Andrea. They decided to record the song in a reggae style more representative of the music that people in Korogocho listened to. The group recorded shots all around Korogocho. They used caution where they used the camera because parading expensive equipment around the slum would attract the attention of gangsters. They took shots of Grogon Road and Dandora dumpsite from a distance to stay out of the way of potential harm.

After recording the song, Andrea edited it and presented it to Daniel. Daniel was glad to have something to get to Father Moschetti so he could take it to his meetings in Europe. Andrea suggested to Daniel that he post the song on YouTube. Daniel had never posted videos online and did not have internet access; Andrea offered to post the song for him.

The Hope Raisers were nervous and ecstatic about publicizing their video. They did not know how the internet worked or how many people their song could actually reach. Daniel guessed it would be heard by a few dozen people—but he was wrong. The "G8" song reached thousands of people around the world after Andrea uploaded it.[1] As the intensity of the campaigns for dropping Kenya's debt continued to build, the "G8" song garnered a lot of attention. It was shared among nongovernmental organizations and was even presented at the World Social Forum. As he had dreamed of doing, Daniel was suddenly making an impact through his band.

Mutura returned home to Korogocho from school, astounded to see that his closest friend had become a celebrity. He wished he was an official member of the Hope Raisers but was grateful to be involved in their practices and for the success of his friend. Mutura provided encouragement and new ideas about how the band could make a bigger impact. He knew the Hope Raisers were something special. They created a platform for real change from nothing, and he was determined to contribute to it, even if in an unofficial capacity.

In October 2006, the historic deal that the Hope Raisers fought for became reality. The Italian and Kenyan governments agreed that the 55.7 million U.S. dollars owed to them would get redistributed for improving health, water and irrigation, urban development, and education across slums in Kenya. Father Moschetti leveraged the message of the Hope Raisers' "G8" song and the strength of his relationships with the government officials to ensure that Korogocho was one of the beneficiaries.

The debt-swap initiative between Italy and Kenya became known as the Kenya-Italy Debt for Development Programme (KIDDP). The Korogocho Slum Upgrading Programme (KSUP) was born out of the KIDDP. For once, the future of Korogocho seemed bright. Residents were full of hope.

Unfortunately, it was only a matter of time before the Korogocho Slum Upgrading Programme became an embarrassment.

CHAPTER FIVE

A Failed Upgrading Program

The Hope Raisers (from left to right: Isaiah, Simon, Robert, Daniel) perform at the 2007 Pan-African Youth Forum in Nairobi. They were invited to many such events following the popularity of their "G8" song, which inspired Daniel to empower children throughout Korogocho in harnessing their creative abilities. COURTESY OF HOPE RAISERS

DUE TO THEIR INFLUENCE ON PUSHING THE KENYA-ITALY Debt for Development Programme, the Hope Raisers became a national sensation. Instead of seeking out audiences, they were invited to perform at global development forums and social impact shows. The most exciting invitation was in Germany, but unfortunately, Daniel and his band could not get passports in time to attend.

The "G8" song also spread through other mediums. Daniel heard it on one of Kenya's most popular reggae radio stations, Metro FM. Sometimes people told him that they saw his video on television. The amount of attention scared Daniel slightly. He expected some short-lived support until the novelty of the song wore off, but news about the Hope Raisers kept spreading.

Daniel became an ambassador with an obligation to spread messages about the eradication of poverty, life in the slums, and conflict resolution. He attended development forums to bridge the connection between impoverished communities and the world outside. The forums taught him that there were numerous avenues to propagate messages beyond music.

This made Daniel realize the larger opportunities that lay in front of him and the Hope Raisers. He thought he might be able to empower others to harness their creative abilities. Enabling such a solution would further the reach and impact of the Hope Raisers' messages. Daniel started planning art and music classes at St. John's. From the beginning, kids around Korogocho loved the activities. They felt they had a real voice, instead of the one that remained stifled.

The success of the classes proved to Daniel he could do even more. He organized a festival called Koch Fest where local artists showcased their skills. A roadblock he ran into was the administration at St. John's. The church was a hub for all of Korogocho, and other community-related initiatives also had to take place. There was not enough space for everything, so the administration did not approve all the activities he wanted to set in motion. Daniel made the decision to separate the Hope Raisers from the church. This would allow them to partner with other organizations and host their activities in more locations. He registered the Hope Raisers as an independent entity— a community art–based organization with the mission of creating a safer community and providing opportunities for people to better their situations. To live up to the mission of being more than just a band, Daniel needed assistance. The first person he thought of having help him was Mutura. His open-mindedness, dedication, and visionary perspective on the community would be a valuable asset.

The timing of the decision to expand coincided with Mutura's graduation from high school and his return to Korogocho. As soon as Mutura arrived back in the slum, Daniel explained what he wanted to do to expand the Hope Raisers' efforts outside of music. He asked Mutura to help. Mutura accepted without hesitation.

Growing the Hope Raisers' initiatives was far from easy. Activities that could not be accommodated at St. John's moved to the streets, which became the new home of the Hope Raisers. Kids danced and painted out in the open. But the streets of Korogocho were not optimal.

In early 2008, violence broke out around the slum following a controversial presidential election. Rumors swirled of voting manipulation. It led to an outbreak of tribal and ethnic violence. The day the election results were announced, Daniel and Mutura were painting with some kids in the streets when they heard a loud explosion from the direction of Ngomongo. Worried about the safety of his mother, Mutura convinced Daniel to go with him to Ngomongo. A friend there had electricity and a TV, so they could check on Mama Bonie and monitor the news.

Mama Bonie was huddled inside their house to avoid the tribal violence. She encouraged Daniel and Mutura to stay with her when they turned around to leave.

"We are going to our friend's house close by. I promise we will stay inside there," Mutura assured her. This seemed to calm Mama Bonie's nerves.

Daniel and Mutura stayed at their friend's house for the rest of the evening watching the news. It showed rallies and boycotts forming around the entire country. These quickly turned into gruesome killing rampages.

"We should practice acting like members of different tribes in case we get caught up in a bad situation," said Daniel, mostly joking. Little did he know that this would actually be a useful skill to have.

When the boys turned off the TV and went outside to the streets, people were ready to attack anybody who was not part of their tribe with sticks and machetes. Daniel and Mutura somehow steered clear of the trouble.

For many weeks, hostility remained the norm. The boys had no choice but to abandon all Hope Raisers activities until the situation improved. People deserted the streets. Nobody dared venture outside unless it was in a large group with weapons. Food became unavailable. People had to walk 5 kilometers (3.1 miles) from Korogocho to find the nearest vendors.

With thousands of lives disrupted and no obvious resolution, mediators from the United Nations intervened. They mobilized leaders to bridge the divide between tribes. Then, they began to work toward long-term solutions to the poverty, inequality, and unemployment problems. Government officials agreed to use funds from the Kenya-Italy Debt for Development Programme. This notion felt promising, and as the violence wound down, Daniel and Mutura restarted the Hope Raisers' community activities. They remained at the mercy of the unstable streets but were hopeful for improvements as the KIDDP funds began to get put to use.

Government representatives held a groundbreaking ceremony to kick off the Slum Upgrading Programme, witnessed by hundreds of buzzing community members. Daniel, Mutura, Mama Bonie, and Lucy were all in attendance. They wanted to hear more about the program and take part in changing their slum for the better.

The representatives from the local and federal government involved in the program knew how important it was to keep residents active in the project. They promised that all decisions on improvements would include the voice of the community. To cement this pledge, they established a Korogocho Residents' Committee (KRC). The committee would consist of six resident representatives from each village in the slum. Elections would be held to select resident representatives.

All were thrilled by the approach, but some residents were skeptical that it would happen as described. They had witnessed grand projects before that had turned into empty promises.

Daniel immediately became a proponent of the initiative, convinced it would be better than anything done in the past. He saw that there would be an effort to run the program with local organization this time and that the Slum Upgrading Programme represented the people of Korogocho. He used his strong conviction and relentless optimism to convince or exhaust skeptics.

The resident representatives for the KRC were elected with great fanfare. They were mainly senior or well-known residents from each village. For the first three months, community members came to them, enthusiastically providing them with input. Daniel and Mutura offered suggestions of their own, such as locations for the construction of footbridges that would connect Korogocho to surrounding municipalities and create opportunities.

As the Slum Upgrading Programme unfolded, it began to move down the path of past programs. The KRC representatives said that they encouraged feedback but did not bother to listen or take action on most of the community members' concerns or suggestions. They failed to be the voice of the community in delivering ideas and concerns to the government officials.

Because of the lack of input from the KRC, government officials started defining and implementing their own improvements in Korogocho. Some residents alleged that representatives in the KRC did not care to push back because of the opportunities to profit by letting the politicians take control. The federal government provided funds for selected changes and relied on the KRC to put projects in motion. When KRC representatives received the money, they skimped on estimated resources that they would need. They hired cheaper laborers and contractors and pocketed whatever remained. It was an easy and effective scheme.

When it came time to vote for new KRC representatives, the original members simply refused to step down. They converted the committee into a community-based organization, exploiting a loophole that did not require leaders to get reelected. In a country where corruption is commonplace, it would have been a surprise to have a democratic voting system succeed. It was a lack of foresight by government officials to think that it might.

What started off as a committee to channel input on behalf of the residents turned into an organization of self-interest and corruption. Members of the KRC rose from low-class to middle-class citizens and grew out of touch with their neighbors. Daniel and Mutura heard rumors that they urged the government to plan bigger projects so they could capture more of the profits.

Eventually, the government representatives approved the biggest project of all: street renovations. This included paving roads, adding a drainage system, and installing streetlights. Government officials thought that paved roads would connect Korogocho with surrounding estates and Nairobi. Residents of Korogocho felt that their social status effectively banished them from such areas. New roads could not solve the indignities they faced. None of them owned cars, mopeds, bicycles, or even skateboards. Though most residents did not see value of paving the streets, the upgrades still began.

This type of misunderstanding of local issues echoed previous projects. Various organizations and charities came to Korogocho with plans to transform the community. Their leaders were far removed from the experience of slum life and couldn't understand its key cultural, social, and economic dynamics. They did not spend time with the community members to learn about the actual problems. The projects ended up either failing or having limited impact. Residents were grateful for the time and resources that volunteers sacrificed. But each time, the effort and resources resolved nothing. Connecting with people and investing in them rather than extravagant projects would make a greater impact.

For example, a few years before Mutura dropped out of school, a foreign nongovernmental organization started a campaign to help prevent the spread of HIV and AIDS. Volunteers began plastering signs all around Korogocho about the dire consequences of the disease, meant to scare residents. The signs were similar to the striking pictures and messages seen on boxes of cigarettes. The root of the problem was not that people in Korogocho were unaware of the dangers of HIV and AIDS. The problem was that they didn't know what HIV and AIDS was, how it was contracted, and how to avoid it. Most teenagers in the slums didn't even know these diseases spread through sexual contact. The volunteers never checked what they thought was obvious, incorrectly assuming the means of transmission was common knowledge.

The campaign ultimately had minimal impact. HIV and AIDS continued to pose a major problem in Korogocho. Speaking to some of the teenagers in the slum would have revealed that signs were not going to help. Condom distribution and sexual education programs would be more effective. Members of the organization probably would not have witnessed the benefits of their hard work while in Korogocho. The long-term effort might have paid off, even if progress was slow. Teenagers familiar with these diseases could pass the knowledge on to others over time, slowing or even stopping the spread of HIV and AIDS.

When Daniel was much younger, another example occurred when the leaders of an external food bank arrived in Korogocho, promising that they would solve all the slum's food shortage problems. They dedicated a couple of volunteers to serve meals to the locals every evening. This was not a sustainable solution as it was only creating dependency without opportunity and participation. It wasn't a surprise when the volunteers failed to arrive one day without warning.

In the same way, the street development programs proposed for Korogocho did not invest in the people or address the underlying causes of the issues affecting them in the slum. The initiatives were good solutions for a community with a different set of problems. Daniel and Mutura attempted to convince the KRC to renovate just the main streets and put the additional funds to other uses, such as toward the construction of the footbridges or perhaps even a school. These were realistic solutions that would help the people of Korogocho immediately.

Everyone used the main roads, so there was little benefit in developing the others. The committee went ahead with its plans as they were and renovated all the streets. It put all the money toward building roads to accommodate full-sized vehicles that no one owned. In reality, the streets only needed to be a meter wide, because they were little more than footpaths. Not a single road was built with pedestrian traffic in mind.

Community members criticized this improper use of funds. Before long, their strong dissatisfaction with the Slum Upgrading Programme reached the highest levels of the Kenyan government. Rumors of the lack of success with the program circulated around Nairobi. This piqued the interest of social policy organizations. Researchers from institutions used the Korogocho Slum Upgrading Programme as an example of how not to run a community initiative. They stressed that the lesson to be learned was how important it is to create ongoing local involvement in initiatives. Local ownership was an afterthought in the Korogocho Slum Upgrading Programme.

Daniel tried to maintain a positive outlook, but most residents lost faith in the program and local support weakened. What had started with such promise ended by confirming the initial doubts of the skeptics. While they looked at the program as a failure, an unexpected miracle would come out of those street development initiatives.

Chapter Six

An Unexpected Road

A young boy skates on the newly paved roads of Korogocho while other children watch and await their turn. News of the sport spread so fast that Daniel and Mutura were forced to share one pair of rollerblades among fifty kids. COURTESY OF HOPE RAISERS

The results of the Slum Upgrading Programme left Daniel and Mutura feeling more obligated to offer meaningful creative outlets to youth in Korogocho. They went back and forth between Korogocho and Nairobi to establish relationships with partners and continued expanding the Hope Raisers' initiatives. The boys would take the *matatu* whenever they could afford to. *Matatus* are privately owned minibuses that serve as Kenya's public transport system. The term translates to "three," because when they were first introduced, the fare per ride was three pennies.

Each minibus is covered with eye-popping graffiti or artwork meant to make it stand out from the competition. Riders squeeze into the *matatus* like exclusive nightclubs. Some of them hang off the door if there are not enough seats. Inside, hip-hop or trendy African music blares to enhance the personality of the *matatu* through the musical experience.

Many of the introductions Daniel and Mutura made in Nairobi were facilitated through global development forums where the Hope Raisers band performed. They spoke to and established partnerships with everybody they could. In some cases, they even formed personal connections with the people they met. In return, these people exposed the boys to parts of the world they had not seen before.

Once, one of Daniel's new friends, Isaac Mburu, invited him to a popular park in the central business district. When they arrived, Daniel saw several teenagers whizzing around the park with strange wheels strapped to their feet.

Daniel turned to Isaac. "What are all these people doing?"

"They are rollerblading!" said Isaac.

"Rollerblading," Daniel repeated to himself.

Isaac tried his best to explain. He skated often, and his legs were full of scars to show it. "It is a new sport in Kenya. You try to go as fast as you can and beat others in races. You can do tricks too."

The only sport Daniel had ever played in Korogocho was soccer. It looked like the people participating were having a lot of fun. He thought about Lucy and wondered if athletes like her would enjoy rollerblading. It could give them another sport to play as an alternative and another reason to avoid getting involved in violence and crime.

Besides having no idea whether it was as much fun as it looked, Daniel also had no idea how he would get rollerblades. He didn't know where to buy them and even if he did, he was pretty sure that he wouldn't be able to afford them. He didn't know if it was hard to learn but was interested in trying. Perhaps he could teach himself one day.

On the way back to Korogocho, Daniel found himself thinking about how he could bring rollerblading to the village. No matter how hard he tried to focus on the other ongoing Hope Raisers initiatives, his mind kept returning to rollerblading. There was something special about the sport that captured his interest.

Once back in Korogocho, he told Mutura about the strange sport he saw in Nairobi.

"You wear these shoes with wheels on them and try to race or do tricks," Daniel said.

"Do you think that we can bring these shoes to Korogocho as a Hope Raisers initiative?" Mutura questioned.

"That's what I keep thinking about. I don't know where we would get the shoes or how hard it would actually be to learn," Daniel replied.

"We will find a way. We always do," Mutura said.

Just a few days later, Daniel and Mutura were walking by St. John's. Directly in front of the church was a standing, informal market where trash pickers sold things from the Dandora dumpsite. They piled items in mounds on ragged blankets. For the most part, nothing was organized—it was up to the buyer to sift through everything and find what he or she wanted. Some of the items were useful. Others, like CD players or video cameras, were useless because they were broken or outdated. The trash pickers knew next to nothing about what their items were worth when they put them all out for sale. They hoped more knowledgeable buyers would come by and offer an attractive price.

In one of the piles, Daniel noticed small plastic wheels peeking out from the bottom. They reminded him of the rollerblade wheels he saw in Nairobi. He took a closer look and wondered if those small wheels by chance belonged to the underside of a blade.

"Can I see this, *naeza angalia hii*?" Daniel asked the merchant while pointing to the set of wheels. The merchant came alive seeing Daniel interested in the product.

"Okay, *sawa*, these wheels are the best quality . . . ," he declared, pulling them out from his messy heap. The trash picker's voice trailed off as he realized that the wheels were attached to some sort of boot. It was clear that he had no idea what the item actually was. Regardless, he kept pushing the sale.

"The black color is very nice," the trash picker pointed out.

Daniel could not believe what he was looking at. Here was a merchant right by St. John's unknowingly selling the exact thing Daniel wanted, found and excavated from the Dandora dumpsite.

"Do you have another one like this?" asked Daniel.

"Yes of course," replied the merchant, hesitantly. He started digging through his pile. He did not seem sure he had another one, but he did not want to lose the potential sale. The merchant kept rummaging until he produced another rollerblade. "Here is one more," he said, handing both of them to Daniel for inspection.

Miraculously, the rollerblades were a matching pair. Daniel examined them and tried spinning the wheels. The plastic was worn down and the wheels spun, but very stiffly. He tried them on and discovered that the inner soles were missing. Without the soles, Daniel could feel the hard, uncomfortable plastic inside the boots. The rollerblades were also too small for him; he had to bend his toes back to fit his foot inside. Regardless, he was ecstatic to have found a pair.

He turned to Mutura with the skates. "These are the shoes I was telling you about that are used for rollerblading!"

Mutura had never seen anything like them before. "They look cool," he said.

"How much for these?" Daniel asked the merchant.

"Five hundred shillings," the trash picker responded without taking a breath. He quoted a high price, anticipating additional questions or bargaining like other buyers did before just offering to buy.

Daniel pulled out some money that he had earned from the Hope Raisers' performances. To the merchant's surprise, he handed the 500 shillings (USD 5) over without any fuss.

"Thank you, *asante sana!*" exclaimed the trash picker, hiding the cash before Daniel could change his mind. Daniel tucked his new purchase under his arm.

"Who will teach the kids how to rollerblade?" Mutura asked.

"I suppose it will have to be one of us," admitted Daniel.

During the next few weeks, Daniel took his rollerblades out into the streets and taught himself how to skate. He looked incredibly awkward and uncoordinated at first. It wasn't long before he was able to balance himself, though. With that small victory he was already excited by the idea of being able to speed through the roads. He made a ritual of waking up early every morning and skating on Main Road.

Residents noticed him rollerblading. Some of them laughed at the strange contraptions he wore on his feet. A few asked what he was doing and if he was crazy. Undeterred and making progress with his skills, Daniel continued skating every morning. Mutura eventually joined in. They shared the rollerblades and skated around the freshly paved surfaces without any competition for the road. After practicing hours on end, they would sit around on the roadside and relax.

News travels fast in Korogocho. There is no need for social media or electronics. Kids started gossiping about the two boys playing some type of new sport on the streets. Dozens of children showed up hoping to try it out.

The skills Daniel picked up over the past weeks gave him enough confidence to demonstrate the basics of the sport to the other kids. Daniel made it look so easy that the kids could not wait to try for themselves. They were not watching during the many hours he spent practicing to sharpen his rollerblading abilities.

After the demonstration, Daniel attracted a bit of a crowd. He held up his rollerblades and exclaimed, "Who wants to try first?" The kids fought for his attention, eager to go first. Mutura laughed at the chaos and helped Daniel choose the most well-behaved of the group to take a turn.

"Don't worry, everyone will get a turn!" Mutura promised. That was enough to get the rest of the children to settle down.

The blades were too small for Daniel's feet, but those much younger than him experienced the opposite problem. Improvising, he did makeshift fittings for each child who wanted to try skating, using his own socks to stuff inside the boots. When it came to a child with still smaller feet, he asked Mutura for his socks as well.

One by one, the kids found out that rollerblading was not as easy as Daniel made it look. It took all of them several tries just to understand how to stand and balance with wheels on their feet. Even so, they loved the challenge and did not seem to get discouraged.

The next day when Daniel and Mutura went to skate, thirty kids showed up wanting to try. Both boys were determined to give everyone a turn, even if there was only one pair of rollerblades. They selected the participants to take their turns, again fitting the rollerblades with socks and helping the children attempt to skate. Everyone got to use the rollerblades for five minutes each while they worked on the basics of standing with controlled balance and attempting to make their first strides forward.

In the following days, the number of kids showing up to try out skating exploded. On the third day, fifty kids came out. Daniel and Mutura could see they had to do something to continue to introduce rollerblading to the kids as an official Hope Raisers initiative. The interest was clear, and that pushed Daniel and Mutura to organize formal skating activities.

That night, the boys decided on a plan. The Hope Raisers continued to earn some money from their musical performances. They wanted to use the money to purchase more skates. Because the sport was still in its infancy in Kenya, brand-new rollerblades were too expensive. An unused pair cost at least 3,000 shillings (USD 30). As all the kids were beginners, there was no need for new rollerblades. They would purchase cheaper, secondhand skates from amateurs who had given up.

Daniel scoured markets around and outside of Korogocho to find rollerblades. In a short period of time, he was able to find six pairs. The additional boots allowed more kids to skate for longer periods of time. Still, the rate at which they obtained rollerblades was not enough to keep up with the demand from the number of new kids who were interested in the sport.

Daniel and Mutura sent desperate messages to community members, family, and friends, begging for donations to support their new initiative.

The history of previous projects in the slum marred their efforts. Skeptics thought Daniel and Mutura were just trying to profit under the guise of helping kids learn to skate. They were sure that the boys would disappear as soon as they received any money.

Some parents thought that Daniel and Mutura were being irresponsible for spreading interest in such a dangerous sport. None of the children wore safety gear while skating. If they fell, they could easily bruise themselves, break bones, or experience concussions. Given the lack of available health care in Korogocho, it might take only one injury to ruin a child's entire life.

This resistance left Daniel and Mutura on their own to lead the rollerblading activities without assistance from the community or the children's parents. Managing it sometimes meant getting creative. During summer, when school was out of session, the number of kids swelled to more than one hundred. Not wanting to turn them away, the boys encouraged friends to pair up and skate two at a time with one pair of rollerblades. One person would wear a skate on the right foot, and the other would wear a skate on the left foot and put an arm around their friend's shoulder. They had to keep the foot in the middle off the ground and see how long they could keep from falling down. It was unconventional, but it actually seemed to help the kids perfect their balance.

The group got so large finally that Daniel and Mutura had to search for a place that could better accommodate them all. Grogon Road appeared to be the best option as it was the emptiest street in all of Korogocho. Nobody ventured there because of the gangs. Due to the threat of danger, Daniel and Mutura were even hesitant to take the kids there at first. Some of the children who were from Grogon convinced Daniel that there would be no problems skating on Grogon Road. Gangsters never touched those who lived on Grogon or their friends.

After deliberating, Daniel and Mutura at last decided to go to Grogon. During the first session, the boys nervously kept their eyes on all the bystanders and prayed nothing violent would happen. There was no clear path of escape if they were attacked. They were at the mercy of the gangs. The session passed without incident, and Grogon Road became the designated practice area for rollerblading.

When Mutura told Mama Bonie what they had been doing, she was struck with disbelief.

"You're skating with kids on Grogon Road!? Are you sure it's safe?" Mama Bonie questioned.

Mutura assured her that it was. Such was the impact of rollerblading. It was beginning to trigger an improbable transformation, bringing members of different tribes together on one of the most dangerous roads in Korogocho.

CHAPTER SEVEN

Fat Women Can Skate Too

Some boys sweep away debris in preparation for a skating session on Grogon Road. This became the spot where all the children practiced. COURTESY OF HOPE RAISERS

Lucy heard about rollerblading on Grogon Road from several kids who were attending the practices and boasting about how much fun they were. Even though she knew about the Hope Raisers, she was a bit surprised to find out that Daniel was one of the people promoting it. Her natural curiosity and desire for challenges drove her to venture out and see this new sport for herself.

She was brimming with excitement as she approached Grogon Road and saw the kids who had congregated there. All but one of them were boys. Even reckless girls would have thought participating in rollerblading was frivolous. Kenyan women spent most of their days supporting their families by toiling in nearby marketplaces, the Dandora dumpsite, or anywhere else they could find work. They are expected to bear the responsibility of sustaining their households and caring for children. Because of this, they have double workdays where they do not just relax when they get home, and that leaves them no time for frivolous sports.

From the beginning, Lucy held to a very different mindset. She wanted to go against the norm and prove that she was capable of doing the same things that boys did. She refused to take the path other Kenyan women did and get married just to play a role she was given by tradition. Taking on something that seemed geared to boys made her feel that Grogon Road was the perfect place to be.

Lucy looked around for Daniel and spotted him handing out shoes to the kids. She walked toward him, waved, and called his name to get his attention above the crowd of kids.

"Lucy! What are you doing here? Are you giving up soccer?" joked Daniel when he saw her.

Lucy laughed. "I came here to see this new sport. I have heard about it from a lot of people." She admired how leisurely he was talking to her while continuing to attend to the other kids, as if fitting the shoes was second nature.

"Are those shoes with wheels the rollerblades?" asked Lucy.

"Yes," said Daniel, "those are the rollerblades."

She started asking him questions about the sport, one after the other, like how one kept one's balance, gained speed, or stopped. Finally, Daniel laughed and said, "It is hard in the beginning. If you practice a lot and get familiar with it, it all becomes natural. Do you want to try? We don't have enough rollerblades for everybody but if you wait, you will get a turn," he offered.

Lucy was excited to try it. Just doing it would answer all her questions.

Daniel told Lucy he would call her when he was ready. She nodded and went toward the side of the road where everyone waited for their turn. Mutura joked around with the boys as they passed the time. He greeted Lucy when he saw her and introduced her to all the other kids.

"Lucy is a star," he said. "She is the best soccer player in all of Korogocho."

Lucy blushed, embarrassed by how he was bragging about her talent. "I am here to try rollerblading today!" she said, hoping to focus on what they were all there to do.

Some of the boys did not believe her and made some discouraging comments about girls not being able to skate. Mutura smiled and defended Lucy, saying he knew she would make a terrific skater. He started to talk with her about what she could expect and gave her tips on the fundamentals of the sport, using some of the kids who were taking their turn as examples.

When Daniel called Lucy and said she could take a turn, all the boys kept their attention on her, curious about how a girl would perform. Lucy was much less confident than usual knowing they were watching. She tried to imagine she was just going to play soccer. It made her more comfortable and confident that she could be just as good as the boys.

Daniel helped her get the boots on. When she stood up, she almost lost her balance immediately. She swayed back and forth like a pendulum when she started moving, flailing her arms to try to maintain her center of gravity. A moment later, the rollerblades slid out from under her and she came crashing to the ground. The impact of her hands and wrists on the paved road hurt, but she ignored it and got up again.

This would not be the only time she stumbled. She got the chance to skate for maybe ten minutes total that first day. She tumbled over and over and lost track of how many times she fell. By the end of the session, her wrists and palms were throbbing, but not so bad that it would deter her from proving she could master rollerblading. She asked Daniel when she could come again. He told her they were on Grogon Road every day and that she could come rollerblade anytime.

Lucy went back home that day with a new fixation on defeating the challenge of skating. She replayed the experience over and over again in her head, feeling like she'd already learned something valuable about it.

As she entered Kisumu Ndogo, the sun was starting to set. She veered off the street into one of the narrow back alleys that only locals would know to take. Clothes and tattered undergarments hung from makeshift clotheslines where neighbors put them to dry after washing them in buckets of recycled water. Usually, they took the garments down before it got dark because they could not be sure everything would still be there by morning.

Lucy ducked and dodged her way around the clothing. She jumped over uneven dirt and rocks, making her way through the narrow alley. The back alley was just one of many that was too small to be included in the street renovation project. A shallow trench that formed due to water runoff over the years etched the center. Lucy leaped over it as she moved from left to right in the alley avoiding obstacles. She passed about a dozen shanty structures before turning into one of them.

Lucy pulled back the dirty canvas door flap and entered the house, greeted by the fresh aroma of *ugali* and vegetables. Jackline, her foster mother, hunched over a large tin pot, mixing *ugali* to the perfect consistency.

Jackline's daughter, Chumbana, squealed, excited that Lucy had come home. She looked up to Lucy like a big sister.

"Lucy!" she exclaimed. "What did you do today?"

"I went to eat chicken," joked Lucy, knowing there was no other food Chumbana loved more. She tried to maintain a straight face as Chumbana's eyes widened in disbelief.

"Where did you go? Did you bring me back any?" Chumbana badgered. Chicken was so expensive that she never got a chance to eat it outside of special occasions like Christmas or her birthday.

Lucy broke out laughing, unable to maintain her act. "I am just teasing," she admitted.

Chumbana scowled. "You liar!" She punched Lucy on the arm. Lucy could not stop laughing. "What did you really do?" probed Chumbana again.

"I already told you. I ate chicken," Lucy said with a snicker.

Chumbana punched Lucy again. "Tell me the truth!"

"Chumbana! Behave!" yelled Jackline. Chumbana fell silent and avoided eye contact with her mother. When her mother got angry with her, she knew not to continue. Her punishment hung right above her head tucked in between two tin sheets that made up the ceiling of their home. The red plastic handle of a bucket loomed there as a constant reminder to behave. There were seven of them in different places around the house, so they were handy whenever her mother needed them.

These plastic handles are notorious in the slums. Parents take them from old buckets specifically to discipline children. The handles lie flat when detached from the buckets, making them ideal to use for spankings. For some reason, parents all have the same red tools dedicated for punishment. Kids in Korogocho refer to them as "Mr. Red." If somebody brings up Mr. Red around a group of children—even as a joke—it strikes fear into them and some will run away.

Lucy felt bad that she coaxed Chumbana into trouble with her mom. "I went rollerblading today," she revealed.

Chumbana asked Lucy what rollerblading was while stealing glances at her mother to make sure she would not get in trouble for talking. Jackline was back to focusing on the *ugali*.

"It is a new sport I am learning. You have to wear boots with wheels on them and try to go as fast as you can," Lucy explained. "Daniel and Mutura organize it."

"That sounds dangerous!" interjected Jackline. "What happens if you get hurt? Why did Daniel and Mutura bring that to Korogocho? Did they ask you for money to try it?"

Lucy was expecting Jackline to have a reaction like that because she was protective, especially of her children's safety. "I am being very careful and learning slowly," Lucy said. She did not dare mention the pain in her palms and wrists; otherwise, Jackline would have tried to forbid her from skating again. "Daniel and Mutura brought rollerblading here for fun. They have not asked me for any money. It's free and there are lots of kids doing it."

"Where did they get the rollerblades from?" questioned Jackline, still doubtful.

"I think they bought them with their own money. They only have a few pairs, but they share with everybody," Lucy said. "Chumbana, they will let you try too if you want to come with me when I go next time. It's fun!"

Chumbana shook her head. She was taking karate classes from a neighbor in Kisumu Ndogo. Her mother enrolled her in the classes so she would know how to protect herself against men. Jackline went to the rich estates outside Korogocho to clean houses so she could make extra money to afford Chumbana's classes. Chumbana enjoyed them, and she appreciated being able to stand up for herself. She was not willing to give that up for some new sport she had never seen before.

Lucy did not push the matter further. "I'll keep skating. One day you should come at least see," she told Chumbana.

Lucy spent all her free time at Grogon Road skating with Daniel and Mutura over the next several weeks. She became so addicted to the challenge that rollerblading offered that doing it just once a day was not enough for her anymore. Lucy asked Daniel if she could use the rollerblades outside of practice time. Daniel did not mind. He respected her passion and wanted to see her succeed. Lucy began taking the rollerblades and skating on her own at night.

Being on Grogon Road late at night, especially as a girl, was risky. It could lead to bad situations, rape, or death. If Jackline knew what Lucy was doing, she would have never allowed her to go. Having a stepbrother involved in a gang provided a few benefits, one of which was protection on Grogon Road. Because Lucy's stepbrother was around to watch her, he could make sure she was safe at night.

He did nothing to prevent verbal abuse, however. Gangsters saw Lucy and made fun of her, questioning why she was skating. They told her she was wasting her time because rollerblading was for boys. Lucy did not care who rollerblading was supposed to be for. She was determined to do it, and nothing would stop her.

The gangsters did not appreciate her defiance and resolve. Out of spite, they abused her even more by calling her names. "*Mamayao!* This sport is for athletic kids. It is not for fat women like you," sneered Tiger, a Gaza gang member Lucy had seen at Dandora before. Being called *Mamayao*, a derogatory Swahili slang term used to insult women who are larger in size, hurt Lucy. She did not mind the other things people said, but *Mamayao* made her feel humiliated.

Daniel heard about how the gangsters on Grogon Road taunted Lucy. He urged her to ignore them and keep practicing. The gangsters didn't know what it was like to work hard at something and succeed. Their criminal activity would never take them anywhere.

Daniel's words kept Lucy going. She would not let the gangsters drag her down.

In a few months, Lucy's discipline and consistency in practicing every night started to pay off. She built up her skills and became one of the best skaters in Korogocho. Her ascent pushed the boys to start taking the sport more seriously. Ironically, they needed to work hard to become as good as Lucy now.

Daniel and Mutura never expected rollerblading to become such a success with the kids. They brought it to the village as an alternative activity for children in Korogocho. The interest in skating wasn't limited to just the slums. Daniel heard that rollerblading was becoming something bigger around the rest of Kenya. Kids were taking it so seriously that some skating competitions were organized. Daniel wondered whether skaters from Korogocho were good enough to compete with the outside world. He started to look more seriously at the competitions.

CHAPTER EIGHT

Emergence of a Skating Team

Sellers line both sides of the road at Soko Mjinga market, offering everything from vegetables to clothes. Children bought tomatoes from the market and resold them throughout Korogocho to raise funds for rollerblading. COURTESY OF NIHAR SUTHAR

As DANIEL HEARD ADDITIONAL INFORMATION ABOUT COMPE-
titions being planned from Isaac and another friend Joel
Andanje each time they met in Nairobi, his desire to have the
Hope Raisers participate in them grew. It sounded like many
of the competitors would come from upper-class areas of the
city, and secretly, Daniel wanted to see whether kids from the
slum could keep up with them. He discussed the skating competitions with Mutura, and together they decided to go ahead
and take the next big step in preparation: form an official Hope
Raisers rollerblading team.

There were a lot of unanswered questions. They didn't know
a single thing about how to compete. They didn't know the
level of competition or how skilled kids from rich estates might
be. They didn't know how they would raise the funds to participate. They didn't know how or where to get better rollerblade
equipment meant for racing. They didn't have any real criteria
for selecting members of the team or a tryout process. They just
decided to invite some of their best skaters to join.

Having shown her strength at skating, Lucy was one of the
first people they asked to join. They told her about the skating
competitions being planned around Kenya. She was excited
by the opportunity and agreed. Daniel and Mutura gathered a
handful of boys to join alongside her.

After the full team was assembled, Daniel and Mutura
made skating sessions on Grogon Road mandatory. If the
Hope Raisers wanted to have a shot at proving themselves
against the wealthier kids from Nairobi, they would have to be
in top shape.

One of the first competitions Joel encouraged Daniel to
attend with the Hope Raisers was the Kasarani Skating Championship. It would take place near Korogocho with affordable
entry fees of 200 shillings (USD 2) per skater. Daniel and
Mutura determined that they would be able to pay half of the
entry cost for each skater with money from the band. The rest

would have to come from the rollerbladers themselves. Unfortunately, this forced the boys to start charging fees.

Many parents became irate as soon as Daniel and Mutura asked for money. This was what some were skeptical about from the beginning. None of the kids had even seen competitions. Parents would not justify paying fees for something that could easily end up being a big sham when they were struggling to afford basic necessities.

Some of the team members took it upon themselves to raise the money for their fees. One creative way they discovered to do this was buying and reselling. Korogocho's central shopping area was known as Soko Mjinga by the locals. Soko Mjinga means "foolish market." Nobody knew where the term originated, but everybody agreed that it was the perfect descriptor because all the items, being secondhand, were foolishly cheap. Residents could find anything and everything and would go to buy clothes, do their grocery shopping, or buy decorations for their homes.

Soko Mjinga had the feel of a flea market but was more chaotic, like an auction. Sellers set up goods they had to offer wherever they found a space. Vendors who did not own permanent shops piled their items up on large, dirty canvas sheets along the sides of the road.

Most of the residents who lived near the market were low-class merchants. They were given the land by President Daniel arap Moi expressly for the purpose of starting the local market. The village where the vendors settled became known as Nyayo. This name was a tribute to Moi, who built the premise of his entire presidential campaign on the slogan "Harambe Nyayo." The phrase meant that everyone in all economic classes or tribes could follow in his footsteps to create a better Kenya.

Soko Mjinga market was close to Lucy and Chumbana, so they both went there sometimes to browse. One morning they arrived as the merchants were unloading wooden bullock carts full of goods they had acquired from rural villages nearby. The merchants traveled to these areas to purchase vegetables and other items cheaply to resell at the market in Korogocho.

Some of them, exhausted from their early morning trips, napped on their bullock carts until the crowds of customers began to form. Others took every opportunity to try to sell their goods to anybody passing by. The more aggressive sellers were mostly the merchants who did not have permanent shop fronts at the market. Because they were only there for short periods, they had to make the most of their time selling whatever they could.

Various sellers yelled out to Lucy and Chumbana as they walked through the market looking at the wide selection of goods. They offered deals on items like garments and shoes to the girls. At one of the clothing vendors, Lucy spotted Mama Bonie. She was bargaining over the price of a shirt. Lucy had not spoken to or seen her at the dumpsite in quite some time.

"Mama Bonie!" called Lucy. "What are you doing here?"

Mama Bonie was happy to see Lucy and explained what happened after her hand injury. She mentioned that she started a small business buying and selling clothes. She purchased many of the garments from Soko Mjinga to resell.

"How is your soccer practice going?" asked Mama Bonie. "Have you become the best in Kenya?"

Lucy told her that she recently gave up soccer in favor of rollerblading and joined Daniel and Mutura's Hope Raisers team. This was news to Mama Bonie, but she was not surprised Lucy was motivated to take up rollerblading. If there was anybody who could succeed at a sport like that, it was definitely Lucy.

"I'm already better than all the boys!" Lucy proclaimed, full of pride. "I'm going to get Chumbana and the girls around Korogocho to join me so we can have an all-girls team." Chumbana felt Lucy teasing and frowned.

Mama Bonie laughed and told Lucy she would come watch all the girls skate one day.

As Lucy and Chumbana continued through the market, they came across a merchant with tomatoes for sale spread out on a filthy piece of canvas. Several tomatoes toward the edges of the canvas had splotches of dried mud on them. A massive swarm of flies hovered above the pile. The seller attempted to shoo them away by waving a rag every so often. His efforts were futile. The flies returned within seconds.

Lucy stopped for a moment to glance at the tomatoes.

The merchant instantly tried to tempt Lucy into buying his produce. "These are the best quality tomatoes in Korogocho," he said.

Lucy had no need for the tomatoes and was about to turn and walk off when she got an interesting idea inspired by her conversation with Mama Bonie. "How much are they?" she inquired.

"Seven shillings for three," replied the seller.

Lucy shook her head in disapproval. At this market, everybody bargained. "That is too much," she said. "What is your best price?"

Despite her age, she was not afraid to confront sellers to get better deals.

"Young girl, that is the best I can offer. Seven shillings for three. These are very fresh tomatoes that I just received today," he replied, like a father scolding his child for not having manners.

"How about 3 shillings?" Lucy countered, determined to decrease the price.

The merchant stood his ground. "I already said 7 shillings."

Lucy was not one to give up easily, especially when Chumbana was with her. She had to show Chumbana that it was always better to persevere.

"Name a final price in the middle," she insisted more forcefully.

The merchant shook his head in frustration at Lucy's lack of understanding. "Look, I have to make money from these tomatoes. I traveled five hours to get them. I don't sell them to anyone for less than 7 shillings," he said. "But since you are so adamant, this time only, I will give you three for 5 shillings."

Lucy smiled, satisfied at having gotten her way. "Thank you, *asante sana*. That is a better price. I will buy twenty-one of them." Her plan was to take the tomatoes back to Kisumu Ndogo and other villages around Korogocho. She believed that she could sell three for at least 6 shillings (USD 0.06). That would make a profit of 1 shilling (USD 0.01) over what she originally paid. With twenty-one tomatoes, it would add up to about 7 shillings (USD 0.07) total. Every small profit counted toward her skating fees, and she would not take any of it for granted. A few pennies might be all it took to alter the course of her life.

Later that day, Lucy confirmed that people were more than willing to pay her 6 shillings for three tomatoes. Her tomatoes not only saved residents time from having to go to Soko Mjinga, but they were also cheaper than the usual prices at the market.

She told the others on the skating team about her success in raising money. Some decided to follow suit. They learned that they could get even cheaper prices from the Soko Mjinga merchants if they purchased products before they were removed from bullock carts and trucks. Merchants did not have to go through the hassle of unloading the items, setting them up for sale, or bargaining with buyers, so it made perfect sense for them to offer a discount. Eventually, the team members got to the point where they would put the money they had accumulated together to purchase 400 shillings' (USD 4) worth of tomatoes. Then, they would sell them for 500 shillings (USD 5) around the slums and put the profit of 100 shillings (USD 1) collectively toward financing their skating endeavors.

Lucy also encouraged team members to explore additional avenues of raising money available to them. Another method they discovered was related to the water collection process in Korogocho. There were four large water tanks in the slum that were meant to make accessing water easier. Beside the tanks were small shops where residents paid to collect water. Everybody filled water in the same yellow plastic oil bottles. These bottles were recycled from Dandora and sold everywhere in Korogocho.

Filling a ten-liter bottle with water cost 1 shilling (USD 0.01). A twenty-liter bottle, however, was 3 shillings (USD 0.03). Families usually needed twenty liters of water for drinking, cooking, and cleaning each day. The kids realized they could save 1 shilling (USD 0.01) by filling two ten-liter bottles of water instead of just one twenty-liter bottle.

Through this type of creativity and perseverance, kids scraped together the funds they needed. With the money they raised, the team could successfully sign up for its first competition, the Kasarani Skating Championship, in August 2011. Joel helped Daniel submit the name, information, and payment of each rollerblader to the race coordinators. The team members felt great triumph with what they had accomplished. Unfortunately, it was a short-lived feeling, as the Kasarani Skating Championship would prove to be a vicious introduction to the world of rollerblade racing.

CHAPTER NINE

A Difficult Debut

The Hope Raisers compete at the Aquatic Car Park in Kasarani. Unfortunately, none of them performed well in their first race. COURTESY OF HOPE RAISERS

DANIEL AND MUTURA PUSHED THE HOPE RAISERS TO PRACtice more so they could build their confidence. As the Kasarani Skating Championship got closer, Lucy became increasingly more nervous. She was a proficient skater because of all her sessions on Grogon Road, but she never competed against anybody and didn't know what to expect at the race. Daniel and Mutura heard that the other skaters at the competition, coming from affluent families, would be professionally trained. This made Lucy question whether she could compete with them.

"Give it your best effort!" Daniel urged her. "Just because you are from Korogocho does not mean that you can't compete against wealthy skaters." He assured her that regardless of the final outcome, everybody in Korogocho would be proud of her just for competing.

When the morning of the Kasarani Skating Championship finally came around, Lucy could not control her anxiety. Her heart raced and her muscles tensed up. She was so nervous that she avoided mentioning the competition to Jackline or Chumbana. Usually, she was confident about her abilities, but she did not want them to come watch her until she was certain she could keep up with the wealthier skaters. Lucy simply told Jackline and Chumbana that she was going out to rollerblade.

"Bring back some chicken for me if you find any," joked Chumbana, assuming Lucy was going for practice.

Lucy laughed and promised she would. Then, she slipped out the door of their flimsy house. Grogon Road was the place where the team met prior to the competition. When Lucy got there, a dozen of her Hope Raisers teammates were already waiting. They looked as anxious as she did or even more so.

After all the skaters had arrived, Daniel gathered them around him. "I know you're feeling tense about the race today. Take a deep breath, relax, and just do the best you can. This will be a historic day for the Hope Raisers, regardless of the final results." He looked at each of the skaters one by one, making sure they understood. "When you come back this evening, it won't matter if you won a medal or finished last place. Everybody in Korogocho will see that you worked hard and made an honest effort at something."

Some gangsters, on their way to the Dandora dumpsite, stopped to hear what Daniel was saying. "People will be proud of you for going beyond the boundaries of the slum and competing against highly trained rollerbladers from Nairobi," he continued. "They'll realize how worthwhile this sport is, and the positive change that can come about in our community from it. We'll gain support for attending future competitions. You will be the leaders everybody will look up to."

"Let's go race!" yelled one of the kids, full of enthusiasm.

Tiger, who was among the gang members, burst into laughter. "How is this *Mamayao* going to race?" he mocked, pointing at Lucy.

"She is a top skater," Daniel defended. "All these kids have worked hard to be able to represent Korogocho today."

"Try not to end up embarrassing yourself," sneered Tiger, walking away.

Daniel turned back to the Hope Raisers. "Ignore him. No matter how good you are or how much effort you put into something, there will always be people waiting to knock you down. The best way you can respond is by staying positive, doing your best, and having fun along the way. Everything else is out of your control. One day, he'll see the success we've achieved." Daniel put his arm around Lucy. "Who's ready to go show him what we're capable of?"

The children cheered, eager to get to the racetrack. "We have a forty-minute walk to the stadium in Kasarani but we're leaving very early, so you should all have time to rest before the races start. Mutura and I will distribute the skating equipment to everybody when we get there. Any questions?" Daniel waited a moment, then urged them in the direction of Kasarani with his arm, as if commanding troops into battle. "Good luck and let's go!"

Daniel's words put Lucy at ease. As the team started walking toward Kasarani, a feeling of determination crept over her. She thought about how Tiger ridiculed her and resolved to prove him wrong today.

The Hope Raisers trekked from Grogon Road through Ngomongo, Lucky Summer, and on to Kasarani. In Ngomongo, Mutura had all the kids stop by his house since it was on the way. Mama Bonie insisted on preparing tea for them to ensure they had maximum energy for the competition. Further onward in Lucky Summer, the kids crossed over the Ruaka River, a small body of water between Korogocho and the wealthier estates.

"Look at how clean this river is!" Lucy looked at the river in admiration. The water was dark green and clouded over, but to her, it appeared cleaner than the Mathare River that ran through Korogocho as there was significantly less plastic and waste floating in it. In Korogocho, they had never seen such a pristine body of water.

The kids continued past the river up a steep, winding hill that led to the stadium in Kasarani. Along the side of the road, plastic bottles, bags, and other garbage was strewn about. Community members from Korogocho sifted through it all, searching for items they could turn in for recycling. They were clever to look there as very few people thought of going outside of Dandora to find better recyclables.

The hill to the stadium was so steep and long that by the time the kids made it halfway up, they were dying to just get to the race. Cars, buses, trucks, and motorbikes effortlessly whizzed by them, puffing smoke into their faces, which did not make them any more energetic. Lucy was anxious to see their destination. She never had a reason to come this way before.

"It's just over this hill," said Daniel, encouraging the group. "We are almost there." He had visited the stadium before and knew the journey might seem endless.

They continued climbing, trying their best not to rush out of impatience. Daniel said it was important to pace themselves so they could preserve as much energy as possible before the race.

As the group got to the top of the hill, they were greeted by the massive structure of the stadium, which seemed as familiar as a spaceship. Loud pop music blared from nearby, welcoming the competitors. Lucy felt the rhythm and gently danced to it as she continued walking. One of the kids saw her and laughed, calling aloud to the rest of the group to look at her. She was unfazed by their attention and found it was actually a good distraction to relieve her tension.

The stadium got bigger and the music got louder as they got closer. The parking lots outside the venue were already filled with endless rows of cars. Skaters weaved their way through the parked vehicles, warming up for the races.

The main stadium in Kasarani, known as Moi Stadium, could accommodate more than sixty thousand people. It stood majestically behind the Aquatic Car Park, one of the parking areas where the rollerblading competition would take place. Lucy overheard some skaters saying that this stadium was where the Kenyan national soccer team played its international soccer matches. She imagined being a professional soccer player, competing for her country fueled by the roar of sixty thousand loyal supporters. She felt she left that potential behind when she decided to concentrate on rollerblading.

Wrapped around the Aquatic Car Park was a rectangular road that doubled as the racetrack for the Kasarani Skating Championship. Usually, its purpose was to alleviate traffic going in and out. Today, it was cleared of all obstacles in preparation for the rollerblading competition. The Kenya Federation of Roller Skating (KFRS), the federation governing all roller sports across Kenya, organized everything. The federation was founded by four members. As the popularity of rollerblading grew across Kenya, the KFRS grew along with the interest and became more active in planning competitions. Administrators preferred Kasarani as a location for rollerblading races because of the abundant space.

Daniel and Mutura led the team to an area where the check-in desk was located. Dozens of skaters from various clubs and teams around Kenya had already congregated there. Lucy was surprised at their fancy equipment. Skaters' teams had matching speed skating suits and rollerblades. Lucy did not even know suits like that existed. She was dressed in a pair of old shorts and a T-shirt. None of the Hope Raisers had even thought about the speed advantages they could gain from dressing differently. Most of them were wearing everyday jeans, which would constrict their movements and slow them down.

While skaters from other teams inspected each other's rollerblades, Lucy tried to see what brand of blades they were using. She was able to make out the "Powerslide" on one set of skates. Lucy had heard about Powerslide rollerblades before but never knew what they looked like. These blades had smooth, large wheels and looked like they were made of a lightweight material. It was rumored that Powerslide rollerblades were 100,000 shillings (USD 1,000) per pair. She had never seen that much money in her life. All she could do right now was dream that one day she would be able to afford such exclusive equipment.

The Hope Raisers were still sharing whatever equipment they had. To maximize the number of rollerblades, Daniel and Mutura brought along some plain old boots they found. They took two wheels from each of the rollerblades they already had and attached them to the old boots to make additional pairs of skates. All the rollerblades the Hope Raisers were using only had two wheels on them instead of the usual four, and this would pose another disadvantage for the team.

The announcer's voice boomed over the speakers, inviting the skaters to warm up. The kids from the Hope Raisers skating team did not even know what it meant to warm up. They had never bothered to do so before. They usually just started skating.

"Go on the track and skate around like the others," called Daniel to the team.

Lucy wondered if the warm-up counted for anything in the competition. She did not want to risk doing anything that would take away from the chances of winning. She asked Daniel about the warm-up, and he assured her and the group that it didn't count for anything.

"You can just skate on the track to get used to it. Warming up is important because you need to get your muscles ready to race. You will be working hard." Daniel laughed.

"Okay, *sawa*," Lucy said with an uneasy smile.

She got a pair of rollerblades from Daniel and went to the track. Lucy's feet were large enough that she did not have to spend time fitting the rollerblades like the younger kids needed to do. As she skated around the racetrack, she could tell that with just two wheels, she was not moving as fast as usual. She was already accustomed to using extra force while skating since she trained using rollerblades with old wheels. But now, she needed even more if she wanted to have any hope of competing against the girls with Powerslide skates.

After a few minutes, Lucy skated back to where her teammates were. There were not enough rollerblades for everybody to skate simultaneously, and she wanted to make sure they all got a chance to warm up too. She helped a younger boy put them on.

Lucy observed other competitors while waiting for the race to start. Most of them were with elite skating clubs, doing stretches together. She watched, hoping to learn from what they were doing so she could warm up the right way.

A voice resonated again on the loudspeakers, letting the skaters know the warm-up period was over. Like a track-and-field meet, there were dozens of events, categorized by race length and age group. The announcer called for skaters competing in the five-and-under boys 200-meter race, followed by the five-and-under girls 200-meter.

Lucy would be participating in the 10,000-meter race for twelve-to-thirteen-year-old girls. It would be a while before her event was announced, so she spent the time helping her teammates prepare for their races. Lucy assisted them in adjusting rollerblades, fitting helmets, and putting on safety pads. Protective gear was required for all participants to race. Daniel and Mutura only came up with two sets. Hope Raisers skaters were forced to swap both their rollerblades and safety equipment in the short interval between races. There were three or four minutes at most to hand off the skates, adjust them, and ensure that the next competitor made it to the starting line on time.

A younger boy almost missed his race completely because he had such a short span to get ready. By the time he got the skates, other racers were already getting lined up. Lucy and Mutura worked together to help him put the gear on. They did not have a chance to make sure the skates fit him properly. They got him to the line just seconds before the race began. Of course, with loose-fitting skates and rushing around, he did not end up performing well.

Many narrow escapes like this occurred throughout the day. It was nobody's fault. Daniel and Mutura did their best to acquire more equipment for the team to use, but they were just not prepared for the fast pace of the events. With so many races to run, officials were forced to start one event immediately after the other to remain on schedule.

When it came time for Lucy's race, Mutura helped her get the gear on. He encouraged her while they worked to suit her up.

"Don't overthink anything," he said. "You are just as good as all the other rollerbladers out there. Just go and skate!"

There were five other girls in Lucy's race—all veteran racers. As soon as Lucy approached the starting line, they shot her snobby looks.

"This race is for experienced rollerbladers," one of them derided her, looking at Lucy's old skates and tattered shorts.

"I'm supposed to be in this race," replied Lucy, even though she was shaking.

The girl snickered. "Stop lying, *Mamayao*! Fat girls like you can't race."

Lucy clenched her fists in anger. She was tired of being called *Mamayao*. A lady spectating near the starting line yelled, "Just let her race! Look at her, she's not even a skater. She's going to lose anyways!"

All Lucy's spirit left her, and she found herself wanting to cry at the insults. It was one thing for competitors to be abusing her, but that bystanders were doing it too was even more demoralizing. A small part of her wished she could disappear and never come back to a skating competition again. But then a voice inside of her raised her spirit and urged her to reveal to these girls what she was made of. Her hours upon hours of practice on Grogon Road weren't spent to get beat down by some mean words.

Lucy lined up on the starting line, attempting to block out the distractions and harness the power of her rage. Adrenaline pumped inside her. All she wanted to do was take off skating and show those girls she could compete. An official took his place to the side of the starting line. Lucy crouched down, ready to bolt as soon as his whistle blew.

The shrill sound of the whistle filled the air, and Lucy put every ounce of fury into her first strides. She threw one foot in front of the other, picking up speed. Her rollerblades grunted as they hit the ground with all the force she could muster.

Lucy bolted toward the front of the pack but knew she had to try to conserve energy for the long race. On the straight stretches, she let the rollerblades do some of the work, as well as they could roll. On the turns, she pumped with more energy to maintain her position in the group.

Her teammates cheered her on from the sidelines, yelling things like "You can do it, Lucy!" and "Let's go, *Amum!*" They were not referring to her as "*Amum,*" an endearing Swahili term that translates to "Mother," to poke fun at her. Her teammates saw how she helped them all prepare for their races, and they were using the name as a form of affection and motivation. It would later become her nickname on the team as a constant reminder of her strong, caring, and protective nature.

Through the first few laps of the race, Lucy remained toward the front. It actually looked like she was going to pull off a miracle and win. Her anger burned inside her so much that she had trouble maintaining her composure. As she glanced back to see where all the other skaters were, she lost focus on the track ahead, wobbled, and then fell.

The rest of the girls whizzed by. The voice again urged her to keep going. She forced herself to get up and try to gain on them.

Lucy lost too much ground in the fall. Her valiant efforts to recover were futile. She stayed determined to complete the race. She barreled toward the finish, propelled by the cheering of her teammates. Lucy should have placed last but ended up in fifth because one of the other girls suffered an injury and dropped out. All the Hope Raisers ran to congratulate her as she crossed the finish line.

"Congratulations, *hongera*! You persevered and finished the race!" commended Daniel with a huge smile on his face.

"Thank you, *asante sana*." Lucy's lips formed a faint, meek smile. She was not satisfied with her performance, but for her first race ever, she did okay by simply finishing. The fact that she stayed with the leaders until her fall made her know that she could compete.

None of her teammates performed that well. The best Hope Raisers result was third place, achieved by one of the boys. Aside from that, nobody even came close to winning a race.

This competition served as a good learning experience, and all the team members came away feeling that they were capable of doing much better. They would have numerous opportunities to improve in the future as the Kasarani Skating Championship was just the beginning of the string of competitions they would attend. What became obvious was that the Hope Raisers needed better rollerblades and more equipment if they were going to compete with the best of the skaters on other teams.

CHAPTER TEN

Unsustainable Success

The Hope Raisers skating team pictured in Kasarani. The team grew as locals became aware of their success. COURTESY OF HOPE RAISERS

DANIEL AND MUTURA CONTINUED TO RAISE AWARENESS OF their Hope Raisers initiatives. To increase their reach, they invested in secondhand mobile phones with funds from band performances and established contacts who were interested in helping them. They met with potential supporters in Nairobi and requested rollerblades, speed skating suits, safety gear, and small items like wheels. As the Hope Raisers proved they would compete and saw some success in rollerblading, more people and organizations were willing to donate supplies. Supporters from overseas came to visit with their luggage completely stuffed with rollerblading equipment. Receiving better gear and knowing what to expect at competitions helped Daniel and Mutura govern the team's training to further improve results at races.

The locals were aware of the growing success of the skating team. Some of those who were lucky to have access to TVs saw the kids getting attention on news channels. It was so shocking for the slum to get recognition that some thought that it was a type of propaganda. Nothing good about Korogocho ever came on the news. Yet here was evidence of kids from the community competing against the best rollerbladers in Kenya.

More parents from Korogocho contacted Daniel and Mutura to enroll their children in rollerblading. Most of them were the same parents who spoke up against the boys when they first started charging for skating. Now they begged Daniel and Mutura to accept their children onto the team. The success and opportunities they saw rollerbladers experiencing made them willing to overlook the cost and dangers.

The number of requests became overwhelming. Daniel and Mutura wanted to accept all the kids, but other Hope Raisers initiatives they were working on left them no time to organize more training sessions for an even larger group of children. They decided to hand off some of the responsibilities to experienced skaters like Lucy. Her dedication to skating and passion for passing the sport on to younger children made her an invaluable mentor. She paid special attention to the young girls to personally motivate them using examples of what she had accomplished herself.

Rollerblading became essential to the community. In the past, they believed the only option for buying better food, decent clothes, and caring for their families was to join a gang. Rollerblading introduced kids to a world outside Korogocho. Not having ventured out, they always assumed that everywhere else was just as grim as their slum. Traveling to skating competitions, they mixed with rollerbladers from rich estates, showing them what their lives could become with hard work.

While Lucy pushed everybody to give the sport a try, her special project became Chumbana. Lucy urged her to stop her karate classes and take up skating.

"What's wrong with my karate? I'm good at it," said Chumbana.

"You will be even better at rollerblading. We are going to do it together," Lucy responded.

It did not take many conversations to convince Chumbana to give it a try. She was at a point where she was not getting much better at karate, and her competitive spirit welcomed something new. Chumbana's mother also saw that her skills were becoming misdirected. Jackline originally enrolled Chumbana in karate so she could protect herself from trouble. These days, Chumbana used what she learned to avoid punishments by Mr. Red. She even used martial arts around Korogocho to stir up trouble. People became exhausted with her antics.

Lucy took a pair of Daniel's skates, found a big stick, and led Chumbana to Grogon Road. There was no better place to teach her younger sister how to skate than where she learned herself.

When they arrived on Grogon Road, Chumbana seemed a little nervous. "Is it safe to rollerblade here?" she asked.

"It's completely safe. I've been practicing here for a while now and I know a lot of the people," Lucy reassured her. She handed Chumbana the pair of rollerblades and told her to put them on.

Chumbana sat down and pulled the blades on; then she looked up at Lucy, wondering what to do next. Lucy was slapping the stick she had brought with her against her palm.

"What do you have that stick for?" Chumbana asked. She could fend off the stick using karate, but it would be trickier on skates.

"It is to cane you when you make mistakes," said Lucy with a straight face.

"That's not fair!" Chumbana protested. "I am rollerblading for the first time! I don't want to learn if this is how you are going to teach me."

Lucy started laughing so hard that tears came to her eyes.

Still catching her breath, she said, "The stick is to help you keep your balance."

Chumbana was not amused by Lucy's cruel jokes.

"Can you get up on your own?" Lucy said to her.

Chumbana tried to steady herself and planted one foot on the road. It started sliding away before she even got her other foot onto the road. She flailed her arms trying to stand up straight.

Chumbana's struggle reminded Lucy of her own first attempt at skating. She held out the end of the stick and said, "Hold on to this."

Chumbana latched onto the stick and could stand more steadily with its support. Lucy started pulling Chumbana down the road with it. As they picked up more speed and Lucy began to jog, Chumbana held on for dear life. They went about 500 meters, all the way to the end of Grogon Road.

As they reached Ngomongo, Mama Bonie emerged from her home holding a wooden basket full of clothes at her side. She called out to Lucy. "You recruited Chumbana onto your girls' team after all!"

Lucy laughed as she tugged Chumbana forward. "She's the first member! We're going to become the best rollerbladers in all of Kenya."

"I can't wait to watch you win one day!" Mama Bonie said, encouraging them.

Chumbana had a long way to go before she was going to be competitive. Jackline, wary about rollerblading from the beginning, showed concern every time Chumbana returned home with new bruises. Her skin was sensitive, and the scrapes sometimes remained as permanent scars. Lucy knew well that scrapes and bruises were inevitable. It was a small sacrifice to make in the pursuit of becoming the best in Kenya.

Lucy motivated Chumbana to practice daily on Grogon Road for several weeks. Chumbana improved considerably in a short amount of time, enough that Lucy was surprised by her natural talent. Lucy thought that Chumbana could be much better than she was herself. Training grew increasingly rigorous, and while teaching, even Lucy became a better roller-blader, staying ahead of Chumbana's skills.

Lucy signed herself and Chumbana up for every rollerblading competition that Daniel and Mutura scheduled for the Hope Raisers team. The girls' results steadily improved through these races. As news of their success in the competitions spread, an influx of girls came to the Hope Raisers to stand up against the traditional roles of women. The movement started to separate this generation from ideas of early marriage or resorting to lives of crime. Some could not afford the skating fees, but if Lucy thought they were serious enough, she took them under her wing and found a way to help.

The additional girls put a strain on the Hope Raisers' limited supply of equipment. Not only was there not enough equipment, but what was there got more use. Whatever came from gracious donors was never sufficient. Most rollerblades lasted only a year with regular use. Because more people were using each pair, the equipment wore out in just a few months.

Daniel and Mutura saw the problem escalating and set up a campaign to push for donations. They spread the word about how important rollerblading became to Korogocho. Lucy contributed her experience with how rollerblading affected her own life and the girls she was training.

Though the boys increased efforts to expand the program, they found that even long-established donations were not guaranteed. Several partners who provided rollerblading equipment in the past could no longer afford to send it. At the same time, Daniel and Mutura lost a recurring grant from the Italian partner organization they came to rely on. The organization provided 100,000 shillings (USD 1,000) yearly. It provided half of the grant at the beginning of the year, and then it delivered the rest midway through the year.

The boys put that money toward purchasing new rollerblading equipment for the team. While they appreciated the funds, the organization's terms became more unrealistic. In 2013, the partner requested that the Hope Raisers send stories depicting poverty and sadness in the slums of Korogocho. But Daniel and Mutura wanted to focus on the positive part of what rollerblading brought because that was the entire premise behind what they were doing. Ultimately, they refused to send sad stories. Members of the partner organization became infuriated at not having their request met and stopped sending the funding. Daniel and Mutura felt that sacrificing some money was better than sacrificing the core of their mission.

The lack of those funds threw the Hope Raisers skating team into a dark chapter. Without donations, there was no way to purchase new rollerblading equipment, and they had trouble finding any alternatives. Through 2013, the team fell into heartbreaking disarray and lost all the momentum it spurred. The girls got hurt the most, and many of them became disillusioned. Lucy still tried to motivate them to stick with skating despite her outlook for its future. For the first time, she was unsure if she wanted to continue going through the constant struggle of scraping money together to pay her fees.

Chumbana remained optimistic and encouraged Lucy. "We will try our best. We can share our skates. If we are missing wheels or parts, we can find them and fix the skates." She was clearly dedicated to doing whatever it took to keep working at the sport.

Chumbana's positive attitude boosted Lucy's mood, and she vowed not to abandon her girls. Most of them who continued to come and skate were willing to wait as long as it took to get a chance to rollerblade again. Others got fed up and left the team.

Those who were prostitutes or members of gangs prior to rollerblading went back to their old ways and some recruited other teammates to join them. Repercussions rung out all around Korogocho. Girls became pregnant. Many got into pickpocketing or stealing. Tensions flared among the residents as the violence increased. One boy got killed by an angry mob after a failed attempt to snatch a phone in a nearby estate.

The village chief utilized the events as a platform to speak up about his regrets regarding rollerblading. "In the long run, skating has neither helped our youth, nor has it changed them. It was useless for them to waste their days in a futile endeavor. None of them have the necessary skills. None of them have degrees. None of them are employed. These kids are not generating any income. They are simply relying on donations from people they never met to keep skating. It is not a surprise that they have turned back to becoming prostitutes, thieves, and getting involved in crime. They could not make it with roller-blading, so now they steal food, valuables, or do whatever else they need to survive. Our youth threw their lives away on pursuing this sport."

Parents around Korogocho berated Daniel and Mutura and held the boys liable for the failure of the skating program because of their lack of dedication and leadership. They demanded to know what both of them did with all the donations. The truth was that Daniel and Mutura spent it all on the skating team. They did not take a single shilling for themselves and worked for free because they believed in the mission of the Hope Raisers. Other members of the group, like Lucy, also endured verbal abuse. It was painful to hear their effort condemned, but the boys agreed that the village chief was right about a few of his observations. Rollerblading was not setting kids up for sustainable futures. It was only a temporary distraction from crime.

Daniel clarified the purpose of the Hope Raisers and tried to explain why it was difficult to go professional in any sport. The intention of the Hope Raisers team was not to turn everybody into pro skaters. The idea was to use rollerblading as an avenue for kids to see another world outside Korogocho and inspire them to dream bigger rather than just surrender to life in the slums.

The boys realized that there was more that they could do to fulfill their mission. Competitive skating provided meaning to many children's lives, but it was just one piece of the puzzle. They had to make some adjustments to the Hope Raisers initiatives to be sure that the kids involved set up sustainable futures.

CHAPTER ELEVEN

Aspirations beyond Skating

Lucy (fourth from the left) after winning first place at a rollerblading competition in downtown Nairobi. Chumbana also came out victorious, and together they inspired the younger girls with their gold medals. COURTESY OF KENYA FEDERATION OF ROLLER SKATING

DANIEL AND MUTURA WORKED ON CHANGES TO IMPROVE THE goals for the skating team. The most important was requiring every member to be actively enrolled in school. If a skater left school, he or she could no longer participate in the Hope Raisers. It was an insurance policy that made rollerblading committed to a positive outcome.

Lucy talked with kids about her professional aspirations outside of skating as she coached. Her dream of being a flight attendant was something she had to explain because most of the girls were never on a plane before. Even though Jomo Kenyatta Airport was just thirty minutes away from Korogocho, they may never have even seen one.

Lucy only heard of flight attendants through the magazines she found around Dandora. She knew nothing about flying, but something made her feel she would be happy making sure all passengers were taken care of properly. Hospitality was part of the Kenyan culture. Strangers will always invite you into their home for a meal. This was the kind of character needed for a good flight attendant.

The nonstop travel also thrilled Lucy. She dreamed of seeing what was outside of Korogocho, and being a flight attendant would allow her to do exactly that. Her hope was to fly with Qatar Airways because she saw a lot of Qatar Airways advertisements in the magazines she found. All of them highlighted the airline's comfort, luxury, and top-tier service.

Motivated by Lucy, Chumbana decided that she wanted to be a medical doctor and save lives. She was only eight years old, but knowing about the shortage of health clinics and medical staff in Korogocho made her realize how much people needed assistance. The small beginnings of sharing dreams and goals helped motivate other skaters to learn about other skills and disciplines.

Daniel and Mutura pushed the group to accept more responsibilities. If kids were owners in the program, they would feel personally invested. Lucy and Chumbana took control over managing the rollerblading equipment. Other children were given the responsibility of handling team logistics and coordinating practice times.

These adjustments freed up Daniel and Mutura to concentrate their efforts on raising more money. They put together a fundraising group and made plans to request donations from everybody they knew and apply for as many grants as they could find. It took some time, but their persistence paid off. A few nonprofit organizations offered to partner with the Hope Raisers and provide funding toward the skating initiative. Daniel and Mutura provided enough evidence through past success and new initiatives that donors believed the program could change lives. Daniel and Mutura put the donations toward rebuilding their stock of rollerblading equipment.

By late 2013, the efforts were enough to bring the Hope Raisers back from the brink of disbanding the skating team. There were still challenges, but their revived spirit made them feel confident they could deal with those issues.

One problem that surfaced was the more recent introduction of motorbikes in Korogocho. They became a popular form of transportation around Kenya because of their low costs and versatility. The prices dropped as motorbikes became more common, and what was previously out of reach suddenly became a possibility. They were most popular among merchants who used them to transport items between Korogocho and other cities to increase their ability to earn more.

The traffic ended up creating dangers for the skaters. In the beginning, they practiced on Grogon Road because it was quiet and spacious and they could take over the entire road. But bikers went fast and did not notice skaters, and the skaters did not always see them coming. Fumes from the motorbikes lowered the air quality, and rollerbladers coughed and ran out of breath more quickly during practice.

Daniel and Mutura put their minds to finding a better place to practice in safety. When they attended a competition in Kasarani by Moi Stadium, Daniel suddenly had an idea.

"Mutura," Daniel said, looking out over the parking lot full of cars, "what do you think these stadium parking lots are like during the week? Do you think they are full of cars?"

Mutura understood what Daniel was thinking. "They won't be full, except for when there are events! The parking lots are public spaces. Our team could use them if they are empty."

Daniel and Mutura made plans to come back throughout the week to check on the parking lots. If they were unoccupied, the boys were going to announce to the skaters that there was a new space for their practices. It would be good use of an otherwise vacant public area removed from all traffic. The lots were flat and large, perfect for skating, and they would be a better practice spot than Grogon Road.

As Daniel thought, the parking lots were completely empty during the week, and he announced to the skating team that they had a new home for practices.

The only downside of changing practice areas was that Kasarani was a long walk for the skaters. The distance wasn't so important for competitions, which were infrequent. When they started making the walk every day, they realized how far the stadium was from Korogocho. It took Lucy and Chumbana close to an hour to get there. That meant they spent two hours each day just walking to and from practice. Skaters struggled with the uphill portion of the walk, which wore them out. On days where they did not eat much, it was especially difficult to muster the energy to trek up that hill.

As usual, the rollerbladers' resolve kicked in and they discovered a creative solution. The road that led up the hill to Kasarani was a constant bustle of cars, buses, trucks, and motorbikes. Some of the more mischievous girls looked for trucks with extra space in the back and jumped in to hitch a ride as they were driving by. It became a regular routine. The truck drivers probably knew that they had guests. However, none of them bothered to say anything. It was common in Kenya to travel with dozens of passengers in vehicles. Cars meant to seat only five passengers would be stuffed with ten. *Matatus* with a seating capacity of twenty would have more than forty passengers inside and clinging to the outside.

The girls who hopped onto the trucks beat Lucy to the stadium by as much as twenty minutes. When she finally arrived at the stadium, they often pretended to be winded as if they sprinted the distance. They boasted about running up the hill to build stamina. Lucy praised them for taking the initiative to do additional training outside of practice.

"Taking action on your own is how you will become the best at whatever you decide to pursue in life," she said.

They smirked at her responses. The funniest part was that they pulled off the same trick many times without Lucy ever knowing. Lighthearted joking among the members of the group brought the team closer together and made it stronger.

At the end of 2013, Daniel received a message on his phone from a coaching group he was part of. It was an invitation for the team to attend a race at Sunken Car Park in Nairobi's central business district. He accepted, excited for the opportunity to bring the team to a new venue. Entry fees were 200 shillings (USD 2) per skater. Since the team was better funded, Daniel and Mutura decided to cover the registration costs for the skaters. Each person only had to pay 30 shillings (USD 0.30) for transportation expenses on the *matatus*.

Many of the kids had never traveled to downtown Nairobi before. The older skaters looked forward to the experience of riding the bus, but the younger children worried they might get lost. Daniel knew the route well and suggested the entire team ride together.

In the weeks leading up to the race, the kids barraged Daniel and Mutura with questions about the trip. Mutura described the central business district to the curious children. He told them about the most iconic building there, Kenyatta International Convention Centre, known for its unique cylindrical shape. At twenty-eight stories, it towered over every other structure in Nairobi. It was one of the most prestigious buildings in the city, and several senators and government officials had offices in there. The details made the kids more eager to see the city for themselves.

When the morning of the competition came, Korogocho awoke to a torrential downpour. Kenya is notorious for its wet season at the end of every year. The days are full of short, heavy bursts of rain. Lucy and Chumbana thought the rain might affect the event. But as they prepared to leave the slum, the sun began to shine.

Jackline wished the girls good luck on their way out. They navigated through the narrow alley outside their home, circumventing the mud and water runoff from the rain. The Hope Raisers agreed to meet at a bus stop in Kariobangi, an estate neighboring Korogocho just a few minutes past Soko Mjinga market. Daniel and Mutura were there waiting when Lucy and Chumbana arrived. A steady stream of *matatus* flowed through the bus stop with drivers offering rides to a number of destinations. Once the other eleven team members gathered, they boarded one to Nairobi.

Because the Hope Raisers were riding on a weekend morning, the bus was less crowded than usual. They spread out to the window seats so they could see all the sights. Lucy sat near the driver and asked him to play a few songs she knew. She danced the entire way to Nairobi, convincing her teammates to join in to energize them before the competition.

The *matatu* took the Hope Raisers to the city center, from where they had a ten-minute walk to Sunken Car Park. Lavish buildings loomed over the skaters on both sides, and expensive cars packed the roads. It was the complete opposite of what they were used to in Korogocho.

While walking to the racetrack, Kenyatta International Convention Centre came into view. Chumbana remembered Mutura telling them about it and pointed it out as if it was some rare treasure. He laughed, letting her know she found the right building.

The team arrived at Sunken Car Park and the parking area lived up to its name. It rested a few feet below street level. Cleared of obstructions for the competition, the racetrack was marked off with bright tape. Volunteers swept away remaining puddles from the rain to keep the skaters from slipping and getting injured.

Dozens of spectators sat on the stone wall boundaries of the parking lot, awaiting the start of the races. Others stood around, chatting with each other and taking pictures. They were obviously supporters of the wealthier skaters who arrived by car or private shuttle. Some tenants in surrounding apartment complexes came onto their balconies to watch.

Daniel and Mutura started distributing rollerblading equipment to the Hope Raisers members to begin warm-ups. They were used to sharing the equipment by now. Lucy put a pair of skates on and spent a few minutes getting acquainted with the track before passing them on to Chumbana.

As the competition began, Lucy assisted other girls getting their equipment on. She made sure the rollerblades fit well and motivated each of them to do their best before their races. One after the other, the girls fought as hard as they could, but they all came back without finishing at the top of their races. Lucy was proud of their sincere efforts.

The competition slowly progressed through the age categories, getting closer to the one Chumbana was participating in.

"Remember our training," Lucy said, trying to calm Chumbana's nerves. "Today's race is no different than practice. You are as good as the best of these girls," she added, assuring Chumbana that she could win her race.

Chumbana was primed and ready to put her training to use. When her race was called, she checked her gear and made her way to the starting line. Her race was 3,000 meters, or twelve laps on the track.

The whistle blew, and six skaters surged off the line. They fought for position in the pack so they could set the pace. Chumbana got in front of four competitors and stayed on the heels of the skater in first. This skater seemed strong and well trained.

Chumbana knew she would have trouble getting in front. Rather than push to take the first-place position early, she waited and stayed just a few feet behind. She did this on purpose to ensure that the skater in front felt the pressure of someone being on her heels. This made the leader skate faster than she would have liked as she tried to distance herself. Chumbana could tell that the girl was pushing and would tire herself out toward the end of the race.

Ten laps passed with Chumbana right on the tail of the lead skater. As soon as they made it to the eleventh lap, Chumbana stepped up her pace even more. She pushed hard to pick up as much speed as possible. Chumbana overtook the leader, but then the other girl took the lead back half a lap later. Going into the last lap, Chumbana barely stole the lead again.

The rest of the skaters fell far behind. As both girls turned the first corner, Chumbana took the turn a bit wide and her opponent cut inside to take first again. On the backstretch, Chumbana tried to pass, but her opponent battled to stay in front. Coming into the last turn, Chumbana ignored the screaming burn in her legs and accelerated just enough to overtake her opponent.

As they approached the finish line, the girls summoned every last ounce of energy they had. The crowd that gathered at the finish line screamed, urging the girls on. The Hope Raisers team shouted to be heard over the crowd. Even the announcer lost his composure and yelled into the microphone, cheering on the dramatic finale.

Within 20 meters of the line, Chumbana's opponent pulled ahead by less than the length of two rollerblades and the crowd roared. A few meters away from the finish, Chumbana's opponent swayed and crumpled short of the line. Her legs could handle no more, and her body just broke down. Chumbana stayed so focused on finishing that she did not even notice. She kept skating as if the girl she was battling was right next to her and cleanly cleared the line, winning the race.

After Chumbana crossed the finish line, she stopped pushing and put her hands on her thighs, hoping to cool the fire she felt. She realized her opponent was not next to her and looked back to see where she was. As soon as Chumbana took her hands off her thighs, they burned so much that she started swaying and also crumpled to the ground. The six extra seconds of endurance made her a champion. As she remained exhausted and sprawled on the ground, two race officials rushed to her to make sure she was all right.

Neither of the girls were injured. They had just pushed so hard that there was nothing left and they cramped up on a very hot day. After they rested for a few minutes, sipped some water, and slowly skated it off, both were back to feeling normal.

Lucy hugged Chumbana and congratulated her but had to rush to the 10,000-meter race where competitors were lining up. As Lucy got ready at the line it reminded her of the first 10,000-meter race she skated in Kasarani a few years ago. Like déjà vu, some of the same girls were in this race, but Lucy knew she had improved significantly since then.

One of the girls recognized her, called her fat, and pointed out the cheap gear she wore. Another girl laughed at Lucy for continuing to try to skate when she already proved she was not good at it. All Lucy could think was that today was her day. They could make fun of her and say she couldn't skate, but she was not nervous and knew they would have to beat her.

Lucy looked down at her blades. The old plastic pair was still missing a full set of wheels. She did not even look in their direction or at their Powerslide skates so she could concentrate on winning. Confidence and determination seeped out of her.

When the starter asked the girls if they were ready, Lucy nodded and kept her eyes fixed on the opening stretch in front of her. She envisioned herself pulling ahead of the pack. Waiting for the whistle to blow, she took a deep breath.

As soon as she heard the loud shrill of the whistle, she sprang forward. She leaned into her strides and pushed to establish her position in the pack. The ten skaters made the track a little difficult to navigate. After a few hundred yards, Lucy was in last place as all the skaters flew ahead of her in the confusion.

She picked up speed and pulled closer to the pack in front of her. Despite her current position in the race, she made roller-blading look effortless. Her arms and legs moved in a fluid motion. As one of her legs pushed off the ground, the opposite arm swung forward, keeping her body perfectly balanced. She was saving energy while accelerating.

Lucy battled her way into fourth place and kept up with the small pack of girls in front of her. The race was forty laps and for most of it, Lucy held her position in fourth. Toward the thirtieth lap, the girls in front slowed down and let Lucy take the lead. As soon as she took the lead, they pressured her by keeping close behind, pushing her to skate at a faster pace. They were hoping it would wear her out toward the end of the race. Lucy knew what they were doing, but it did not deter her from setting the pace.

On the thirty-sixth lap, the girls who let Lucy take the lead picked up the pace and accelerated past her again. The gap started widening, and Lucy could feel herself losing steam. She reminded herself that today was the day; she put everything she had left into driving forward with the group.

On the thirty-ninth lap, she harnessed her rage and discovered an extra gear she did not even know she had. On that last lap, she soared past everybody and came flying around the last turn in first. She blazed down the homestretch to the finish, not letting up and not looking back. The Hope Raisers team shouted above the crowd, "*Amum! Amum!*"

As she blew through the finish and crossed the line in first, Lucy pumped her arms in victory. It was not even close. She opened up such a large gap that the next skater did not finish until about seven seconds later. The announcer shouted out Lucy's name as the winner of the race, and spectators broke into cheers.

The other competitors did not acknowledge her victory. Still, she was satisfied enough to prove them wrong and show that she could compete with them. Regardless of how they acted, she knew she had earned their respect and the admiration of many people in the crowd as well.

Lucy skated over to her teammates, who greeted her with high fives. Chumbana, thrilled that they had both won their races, asked if they could celebrate with chicken. Neither of them had money to afford that kind of a special meal. They would find another way to commemorate the occasion.

As she sat down to take her rollerblades off, a fair-skinned man approached her. "That was one of the best comebacks I have ever seen! You're a very strong skater," he said in a thick French accent. He wore a crisp-collared shirt and had no hair on his entire head except for a thin goatee. His name was Christophe Audoire, a famous inline coach who founded the World Inline Coach association, a nonprofit organization with a mission to help advance speed roller skating initiatives in developing countries. He searched for and nurtured top talent, hoping to create a movement to add rollerblading to the Olympics.

"Thank you, *asante sana*," replied Lucy. She did not recognize him or know why he approached her.

"I see a lot of potential in you and I want to give you some equipment to reward you for your performance today," he said, offering Lucy a package.

She was glad to win but did not expect a prize. In all the competitions she went to, she had never received one before. She took the package from Christophe a bit tentatively and opened it. To her surprise, she saw a new suit, rollerblades, goggles, and gloves. "Powerslide" was written on the blades.

"Thank you, *asante sana*," Lucy repeated, at a loss for words, staring at her new gear and thinking she might be dreaming. When she was finally able to choke out a few words, she asked Christophe if the Powerslide rollerblades were really hers, believing there might be a reason he would take them back again.

"All of it is your gear to keep as long as you promise to continue working hard at skating," he said. "I think you can win races far beyond Kenya and become a world champion."

The officials conducted an awards ceremony to present the winning skaters with certificates and medals. A few of the Hope Raisers boys placed third in their races, but Lucy and

Chumbana were the only winners. They stood proudly with their gold medals as a professional photographer took pictures for the race organizers to post on the internet. Daniel and Mutura looked on like parents pleased with their children's accomplishments. Other Hope Raisers were ecstatic to see their teammates being recognized.

The team mobbed Lucy and Chumbana as the photographer finished, eager to see the medals up close. Lucy showed hers to the younger girls and let them wear it, encouraging them to keep practicing so that they could win one too. They passed it around, motivated by the idea that someday they could win their own.

Chumbana remained insistent that they still had to celebrate. Lucy looked to Chumbana and started jumping and yelling. In the moment, it was all she could think to do. Chumbana laughed and joined in without hesitation. It was not the gourmet chicken dish she hoped for but something even more rare. Screaming at the top of their lungs, celebrating the improbable odds they beat to win gold medals was pure joy.

Chapter Twelve

Passport to South Africa

Lucy wearing her new Kenyan speed skating suit at a national team practice in Kasarani. COURTESY OF HOPE RAISERS

A FEW DAYS AFTER THE COMPETITION IN NAIROBI, DANIEL got a call from Joseph Mwangi, president of the Kenya Federation of Roller Skating. He told Daniel that everybody was impressed by Lucy's abilities and with her victory. In their opinion, she qualified for a spot on the Kenyan national speed roller skating team. Chumbana also performed well but was too young for the national team as skaters had to be at least fifteen years old. Lucy was a perfect candidate because she turned sixteen right before the race in Nairobi. Joseph explained the details of joining the national squad to Daniel and asked him to pass on the news.

That evening, Daniel walked to Kisumu Ndogo to tell Lucy. She was returning from school when she saw him entering the narrow alley toward her home. She invited him in to eat; Jackline was making *ugali* for dinner and they could share.

Daniel said he only came to deliver some news. "Joseph Mwangi, the president of the Kenya Federation of Roller Skating, called me today. Your race in Nairobi qualified you for the Kenyan national speed roller skating team!"

"They want me to join the national team?" Lucy did not believe it. She wanted to be the best in Kenya but never expected to earn a spot on the national team.

Daniel assured her that the news was true.

She was full of questions, asking for information about the practices and competitions.

He could only tell her that the national team raced against teams from all around the world and Joseph would give her more details during practice.

Practices were every Wednesday, Friday, Saturday, and Sunday in Kasarani at the Moi Stadium parking lots where the Hope Raisers practiced. Since Lucy was in school on Wednesday and Friday, she was only expected to go to practice on Saturday and Sunday. She wanted to start attending the weekend practices as soon as possible, excited about the opportunity to represent Korogocho and her country.

Lucy walked to her first practice the Saturday after getting the news. It felt no different than going to a Hope Raisers session, except that she was by herself.

When she got to Moi Stadium, a very dark-skinned, short, and skinny man was handing out Kenyan national speed suits to skaters in the parking lot. He saw Lucy and waved her over.

"Congratulations and welcome to the Kenyan national team! We're excited to have you join. My name is Joseph Mwangi. I'm the coach. Daniel may have also told you I'm the president of the Kenya Federation of Roller Skating," he said to Lucy, handing her a suit.

"Thank you, *asante sana*," replied Lucy.

There were twenty skaters on the team, four of whom joined with her that day. After they got their suits, Coach Mwangi gave them instructions for the day's practice. They started by doing running exercises and then put their roller-blades on to practice skating techniques. Lucy never ran as part of her training before. Hope Raisers practices focused exclusively on skating.

Coach Mwangi blew a whistle, and everybody jogged around the parking lot as a warm-up for fifteen minutes before switching to more intense sprinting drills. Lucy began to struggle after just ten minutes, breathing heavily, but managed to stay with the others. Coach Mwangi kept barking at the team to increase their pace. His face was stone cold, and his eyes were concealed behind pitch-black sunglasses. He made them run for a total of forty minutes.

Finally, he told the skaters to stop and put their skates on. Lucy slipped on her new Powerslide skates, careful not to scratch them. She could not wait to see how much faster they would make her.

They began skating drills with a technique called the double push. It allows skaters to accelerate faster by pushing from the inside toward the outside with their strides. Coach Mwangi had the team practice the drills for an hour before telling them they did enough for the day.

Ending the session, he shared announcements about upcoming national team events. He said he received a late invitation to a competition in South Africa that started in a week and a half. There was enough time to make preparations and get visas for everyone if they brought their passports to practice the next day. Lucy was not sure what a passport was but did not want to embarrass herself by asking. She thought she would just figure out how to get one overnight.

Lucy walked home from practice, wondering where she could find out about getting a passport. She thought the merchants at Soko Mjinga market might know something about it. As she went down the hill from Kasarani into Lucky Summer, she noticed a small photo studio with a sign promoting its passport services. The studio looked like any other roadside vendor; she'd never needed a passport so she never paid attention to it.

Unable to believe her luck in stumbling on exactly what she was looking for, she went inside. The owner knew everything about passport photos and offered to print all the copies she needed for just 100 shillings (USD 1). Lucy agreed. He took some pictures of her in front of a cloth backdrop, printed them, and cut out four copies for her to keep. She was surprised by how simple everything worked out and could not wait to travel outside Kenya for the first time.

The following day, Lucy took her photos to practice and gave them to Coach Mwangi.

He stared at them in dismay. "What is this?"

"You told us to bring our passports," said Lucy.

"This is not a passport. These are just pictures. We have one week until the race and you don't have a real passport?"

"This is all I was told I had to have," she admitted.

Coach Mwangi sighed. "Okay, don't worry. We will have to get you a passport. Unfortunately, you won't be able to go with the team to South Africa. I can't get a passport made for you in such a short amount of time."

Lucy did not understand what a passport was, what it was for, or why it took time to get one. She hoped it was not too hard to get one so that she could go on the next trip with the team. In the meantime, she was determined to continue to stand out in the national team practices and races she attended with the Hope Raisers.

Chapter Thirteen

Nyali Beach

Lucy (third from the left) helps one of her girls fit a pair of rollerblades before a race in Nairobi. COURTESY OF HOPE RAISERS

ANOTHER RACING OPPORTUNITY AROSE IN APRIL 2014 through the Hope Raisers to compete in the first Mombasa Roller Skating Championship. Entry fees were 500 shillings (USD 5). Transportation costs were an additional 1,800 shillings (USD 18) per skater since Mombasa was more than 450 kilometers (279.6 miles) away. Daniel and Mutura wanted the Hope Raisers to be represented, but they could not afford to send the group to such an expensive competition. Excited about the opportunity, Lucy and Chumbana were eager to try raising the funds and attending on their own.

They did not know exactly how much money they needed to raise or how to organize transportation and accommodations. Daniel had Lucy speak to the owner of the Sky Skaters, Mama Hanaan, who he knew was planning to compete in the Mombasa Roller Skating Championship. The Sky Skaters competed locally around Nairobi, and Daniel had met her at the local competitions. Mama Hanaan was always willing to help rollerbladers around Kenya attend competitions to promote the sport.

Mama Hanaan told Lucy that she would need at least 6,000 shillings (USD 60) to cover the cost of the two-week trip for her and Chumbana. The competition was only four days, but most of the skaters stayed an extra week to explore Mombasa. It was the second-largest city in Kenya, located on the eastern coastline and known for its posh beach resorts and tropical feel. Tourists from around the world swarmed there to enjoy the warm waters, dive among the glistening reefs, and splurge on shopping.

Lucy and Chumbana had never seen the ocean before. Chumbana was excited to experience it for the first time. Lucy was concerned with how they would raise such a large amount of money to afford the trip. None of the competitions they had attended in the past were as expensive as this one. She decided to start off with her tactic of buying and selling tomatoes.

This helped her raise some money, but not nearly enough. She decided to reach out to her family. She did not like asking for money, but this was for her dreams. Her brother heard about the success she was having through skating and helped pay for part of the trip. He even bought a basic mobile phone so she could communicate with race organizers while traveling. Jackline also offered some of her savings to Lucy and Chumbana.

Through this generosity, Lucy and Chumbana raised enough money to attend the competition in Mombasa. Daniel, Mutura, and Mama Hanaan helped them register for the race and purchase bus tickets.

To travel to the competition, Lucy and Chumbana boarded a *matatu* for Nairobi. They rode to the central business district together and then walked to a station near Sunken Car Park where their bus to Mombasa would depart. Lucy enjoyed visiting close to the Sunken Car Park, remembering the gold medals she and Chumbana won there. She wanted to bring back more medals from Mombasa.

The girls had only ever been on *matatus* for short trips in the past. Buses for longer trips like this were much more luxurious. As they stepped onto the bus for Mombasa, they were amazed at how lavish it was. It had very comfortable seats, power outlets, air-conditioning, and television screens. The trip to Mombasa was eight hours long, but felt like it passed by quickly because of the deluxe environment.

When they arrived at the coastal city, the girls were not ready for the drastic change in weather. It was uncomfortably hot and humid. Korogocho was pleasantly warm all the time with temperatures around seventy degrees Fahrenheit. But Mombasa was getting hit by relatively scorching temperatures as high as ninety degrees Fahrenheit with 80 percent humidity.

The race organizers arranged for all the skaters from outside Mombasa to stay at a church with vacant living quarters in Likoni, a suburb southwest of the city. Four people, sometimes from different clubs or teams, were paired together in the rooms. Lucy and Chumbana would be sharing a room with two girls from Mama Hanaan's Sky Skaters team.

The rooms were barren except for beds in each corner. None of the rooms had air-conditioning either. It was so suffocating that the girls slept with the lightest clothes they had and still woke up drenched with sweat.

The brutal temperatures amplified Chumbana's cravings to cool down in the ocean. She reached such a frenzy about the ocean that she was prepared to do whatever it took to go, even if it meant skipping the race.

"First we have to win our competition and then we will go visit the beach," promised Lucy, trying to ensure they did not lose their focus.

The Mombasa Roller Skating Championship took place during the first week of their trip in downtown Mombasa on Mama Ngina Drive. To get to the competition site, the girls took a ferry across the harbor. Mama Ngina Drive was so close to the ocean that the salt smell hung in the air at the competition venue. It took a lot for Chumbana to concentrate on the race, being just a few minutes away from her obsession.

Chumbana participated in some short- and long-distance competitions, starting off with the 5,000-meter. This was the first time she signed up for such a long race. Chumbana lined up, and when the official blew his whistle, she immediately shot by the dozen other girls. They were shocked by her speed. Most of them assumed she was a casual competitor given the old equipment she was using and the fact that they had never seen her in races around Mombasa before. They tried catching up, but Chumbana held the lead throughout the entire race and won gold effortlessly.

When it was Lucy's turn, she was ready to start by showcasing her prowess in the 10,000-meter competition. Because of her new equipment, none of the competitors tried to bully her this time. Instead, they stared at her while lining up, wondering who she was and where she came from. They assumed that she was a rich skater who trained somewhere privately outside of Mombasa. Little did they know that Lucy was from the slums and that after the competition, her big thrill would be going to see the beach for the first time in her life.

This race was the biggest field that Lucy had competed in. There were seventeen other skaters, and she knew establishing her position would be difficult. When the race began, she turned to her usual strategy by lagging behind the leaders of the pack. Then, in the last three laps, she accelerated and overtook them. Lucy came speeding down the final stretch faster than ever before, helped by her upgraded rollerblades. Like Chumbana, she won the race comfortably.

Next, both girls competed in the one-lap sprint, a short race around a track that the race organizers set up. They had never participated in such a short race before, but they both excelled at it and also won.

Spectators and race officials congratulated Lucy and Chumbana for their dominant first-place finishes. Immediately after they received their medals at the awards ceremony, Chumbana looked at Lucy and said, "Let's go to the beach now! You promised!" It was as if their victories didn't matter to her at all.

Lucy tried to encourage Chumbana to be more excited about her wins and reminded her how special they were. "You got first in two races you had no experience with, in a place where you never competed before! Do you know how difficult that is?"

"Thanks," Chumbana said with a grin. "But when are we going to the beach?" When she got focused on something, she would not let the idea out of her head.

"We can go after dropping our equipment off at the church," said Lucy. She had to accept a trip to the beach as a promise she made and another way to celebrate.

The skaters gathered back at the church after the races, discussing the results and what they would do in Mombasa for the next week. Some of them planned to explore the city while others hoped to go to the beach. Lucy overheard someone talking about Nyali Beach; they said it was one of the best beaches to visit. It was only about 13 kilometers (8.1 miles) away from the church. Lucy and Chumbana decided to go there. Before they could leave, though, exhaustion from the competition caught up to them. More than wanting to go to the beach, Chumbana suddenly wanted to sleep. The girls agreed to rest for the night and go to the beach the next day.

In the morning, Lucy and Chumbana took the ferry across the harbor to downtown Mombasa. They asked for directions to Nyali Beach, and somebody told them it was just 10 kilometers (6.2 miles) northeast of the central business area. The girls assumed the 10 kilometers (6.2 miles) to the beach was similar to the distance they traveled to and from Kasarani every day for skating practice, so they decided to start walking.

There was no better day to go to the beach. The sky was bright blue, and the sun radiated its intense heat on the city of Mombasa. As Lucy and Chumbana walked up Mama Ngina Drive, they could feel the fresh, cool breeze of the nearby ocean hitting them. It was unlike anything they had ever felt before. If there was ever a breeze in Korogocho, it was tainted with the smell of waste from Dandora.

Soon the girls became tired, and it seemed that walking to Nyali Beach was taking hours. Lucy asked around and found out that there was a *matatu* that could take them to the beach. The fare was cheap and the ride would take less than thirty minutes. Chumbana laughed as they boarded the bus because she was excited to be close to finally seeing the beach.

Loud hip-hop music blared inside the *matatu*. Chumbana shook her hips to it and nudged Lucy to join in the dance. The girls did not have a care in the world. They were done with their racing obligations and as free spirited as the ocean they were about to see.

The driver announced each bus stop. When they made it to the Nyali Beach stop, Chumbana started squealing in delight, unable to hide her raw emotions. The other passengers stared, wondering if something was wrong with her.

Lucy asked a man by the bus stop for directions to the beach. He pointed and said it was a ten-minute walk to the access point. Chumbana started skipping toward it before Lucy could even thank him.

"Slow down!" Lucy yelled, running to catch up.

Chumbana laughed. "Why don't you move faster?"

As they got closer to the beach access, the paved road turned to dark sand. Chumbana kicked the sand up with her shoes and was surprised how easily it flew into the air. The color of the sand became lighter as the girls walked on, and soon, they heard the sound of waves crashing on the beach.

The sand road opened up onto a majestic view of Nyali Beach with endless, pure white sand. The girls took their shoes off and giggled as their feet sank into it. Chumbana strolled along the shore, digging her soles into the sand, loving how soothing it felt. Occasionally, the girls walked over patches of what looked like dead plants. Some were bright green while some others were darker brown. Chumbana asked Lucy what they were, but Lucy had never heard about weeds being on the beach before and didn't know.

Chumbana examined the plants more closely. She kneeled down and poked them with her finger. A few were dry and bristly. Some others were wet and slippery. Eventually she lost interest and focused her attention on the ocean.

"I'll race you into the water!" she yelled to Lucy. Neither girl had a swimsuit. They sprinted into the water wearing T-shirts and shorts.

Lucy and Chumbana fell down as they went deeper into the pounding waves. They were not expecting the ocean to have such force. They laughed at their clumsiness. Lucy playfully splashed Chumbana with water, and Chumbana returned the favor. Lucy turned away from the barrage until Chumbana stopped.

"How deep do you think this water is?" asked Lucy, trying to distract Chumbana from going on another splashing frenzy.

"I'll find out!" Chumbana said, sloshing further into the ocean. Not far in, she reached a point where her feet came off the ground. Not knowing how to swim, she flailed her arms and kicked her legs, desperately trying to keep her head above the water. She inhaled some of the water and broke into a choking fit. The salty water surprised Chumbana and stung in her throat so much she could not stop coughing.

Lucy yelled out to her, but Chumbana could not stop coughing long enough to reply. Lucy went farther into the water to help, but she did not know how to swim either. She lost her footing, swallowed salt water, and erupted into a choking fit herself. The girls desperately fought their way back to shallow water.

As they got out of the water, a concerned man checked to see if they needed any help. Lucy laughed, admitting it was their first time at the beach. He turned out to be a local merchant who sold fresh coconut water. He showed the girls what looked like a green ball and asked if they wanted some. Lucy and Chumbana had never drunk coconut water before so

Lucy asked what it was. The merchant said everybody drank coconut water in Mombasa and that the city was famous for its coconuts.

Chumbana told Lucy that they could not come all the way to Mombasa and not at least try the coconut water if it was what the city was famous for. In the spirit of their adventure, Lucy got a coconut they could share. They each took a swig of the water inside and hated it. To them it tasted like a mix of salt and dirt. Lucy vowed to never drink coconut water again.

Chumbana knew this would remain one of her most favorite memories even if the coconut water was terrible. Being able to touch the ocean water, feel the fresh breeze, and experience the beach was an image that would be unforgettable.

Through the remainder of their week in Mombasa, Lucy and Chumbana explored the city, public parks, and historic forts. They found some of it interesting and unique, but none of it was as thrilling as the day at Nyali Beach. Chumbana kept talking about the white sand and refreshing waves and thought about the next time she could go back.

At the end of the trip, the girls went back to Korogocho proud and satisfied with everything they had accomplished. When they arrived home, they were welcomed back by the cheers of their Hope Raisers teammates as they all heard the news of the girls' victories.

Lucy thanked Daniel, Mutura, and her teammates for the recognition but reminded them that there was much more work to do. Mombasa taught her that the world was vastly different outside of Korogocho. She shared her experience at the beach and told everyone that she was even more driven to experience new places and become a flight attendant one day. She encouraged them to not lose sight of their vision of the future either. There was more to life than Korogocho.

The Hope Raisers, inspired by Lucy's perspective, focused on rollerblading and school with increased enthusiasm. Chumbana etched the picture of Nyali Beach permanently in her head and trained harder than ever, determined to achieve her goal of returning there as a medical doctor. Perhaps she would even open her own clinic near the beach one day.

CHAPTER FOURTEEN

Adventures across the World

Lucy (fifth from the left) with the Kenyan national team in Guangzhou, China. They had a layover before traveling on to Nanjing for the 2017 Roller Games World Championships. COURTESY OF KENYA FEDERATION OF ROLLER SKATING

AFTER HER TRIP, LUCY ASKED COACH MWANGI AT A NATIONAL team practice if he was able to get her passport. He said the Kenyan government required her parents' written consent and national identity cards since she was a minor.

Being an orphan, Lucy would not have an easy time collecting such documentation. Jackline wrote a consent letter and went with Lucy to the immigration office in Nairobi, hoping it would be enough to get an application started. Because officials could not verify Jackline's relationship to Lucy, they rejected her application despite her pleas.

When Daniel and Mutura heard about the situation, they tried to help. They made an effort to explain Lucy's positive impact in Korogocho as a skater with the Hope Raisers. The officials did not care and instead questioned why so many people were interested in her application.

Without a passport, Lucy missed more competitions with the national team. They got invited to races in Belgium and India that she couldn't go to. Lucy tried to remain optimistic but felt that the situation was unfair.

Being part of the Hope Raisers and seeing her girls succeed kept her motivated. In several races throughout 2014, some of the other girls won medals for the first time. It made them believe their dreams were within reach. Watching them realize successes gave Lucy a renewed spirit that she would still travel abroad with the national team one day.

Lucy turned eighteen years old in 2015 and could finally apply for her passport without needing the additional documentation for minors. She received her pass to travel immediately and began going to international rollerblading competitions with the national team.

Most of the races were initially around East Africa, in countries like Rwanda, Tanzania, and Uganda. The best part of competing internationally was that most races had prize money. Based on her performance, Lucy could win up to 30,000 shillings (USD 300). This was a huge amount to her.

Daniel encouraged her to save and put the money toward her future. As she neared the end of high school, she wanted to start formal training to become a flight attendant. There were many big universities located in Nairobi, so it seemed her best bet.

Toward the end of a weekend when she did not have skating practice, Lucy took a *matatu* to Nairobi's central business district to visit some university offices. She went inside each one to ask if they offered aviation courses. None of the first few she visited did, but one of the university advisors directed her to Nairobi Aviation College nearby. The head office was near the station for the bus to Mombasa.

Inside the office, a bald Kenyan man dressed in a suit and tie greeted Lucy, and she asked about classes for flight attendants.

He said they offered a cabin crew course in the School of Travel & Tourism and they also had many other travel management and airport operation courses.

"Are you sure you want to be a flight attendant?" he asked. "It is one of the most difficult fields to get a job in. Some of our other courses may give you a better chance for a job after you graduate."

"I don't want to do anything else," Lucy said, determined to pursue her dream.

The man asked about her grades in high school; from what she said, she qualified. He gave her the application to complete for enrollment.

A few months later, Lucy received a call on the mobile phone her brother had bought her when she went to Mombasa. It was an admissions officer notifying her that she was accepted into Nairobi Aviation College. Lucy was ecstatic that she took another step in her dream of becoming a flight attendant. She picked up her books and cabin crew uniform at the office in preparation for her classes.

The tuition was 11,700 shillings (USD 117) per month, which made skating competitions and winning suddenly more important than ever. She needed prize money from races to pay. She would need to cover that in addition to paying her Hope Raisers skating team fees, buying equipment for the girls she was teaching to skate, and helping support Jackline.

Her own future, and that of many girls in Korogocho, was on her shoulders. She rose to the occasion and continued to win at every race where she competed.

One of Lucy's most thrilling competitions came in the summer of 2017 when the national team got invited to China for the Roller Games World Championships. Nobody from Korogocho had ever traveled someplace so distant. When news spread that Lucy would be flying in a plane across the world to represent their slum all the way in China, they could not believe she was going. It was a country most of them knew next to nothing about.

Daniel and Mutura coordinated her send-off. Hope Raisers teammates and community members from all over came to crowd the street outside the narrow alley of her home and see her off for her big travel day. They looked forward to hearing stories about her adventures when she returned. Her Hope Raisers teammates chanted, "*Amum! Amum!*"

Lucy was surprised at all the support and came upon Mama Bonie as she walked through the cheering crowd.

"I knew you would be the best in Kenya one day. Now, you have the chance to be the best in the entire world!" said Mama Bonie. Lucy felt humbled because she knew that without Mama Bonie's constant encouragement, she would never have gotten so far. She gave Mama Bonie a hug, and just a step away was Chumbana.

Lucy's star skating pupil was focused on one thing, as usual. "What do you think the chicken is like there?" she said. "Bring some back for me to try!"

Lucy laughed at Chumbana's passion for her favorite food and said, "Next time you will be coming with me so you can try some for yourself!"

Lucy walked away from the jubilant crowd and off toward Kariobangi, where she got on a *matatu* headed to Nairobi's central business district. The national team planned to meet at the Sunken Car Park before proceeding on to Jomo Kenyatta Airport.

There were nine skaters in the travel group—six boys and three girls. Lameck Wafula, the secretary general of the Kenya Federation of Roller Skating, was the leader accompanying the team. He was short and skinny, with very little hair on his head and a thin mustache. His daughter, Sylvia Wafula, was one of the skaters on the national team.

Lameck organized cars to transport the team to the airport. The team members were a bit nervous but excited for the trip. In the car, Sylvia told Lucy about all the teams competing at the World Championships and that there were skaters from as far away as Chile. Lucy had no idea where Chile was but pretended to understand.

At the airport terminal, Lucy saw the massive airplanes that filled the gates, taxiways, and runways. She did not understand how the huge vehicles could even make it off the ground. The only insignia that she recognized from the aircraft was the Qatar Airways symbol. She became more relaxed and excited when Lameck told her the team would be flying on that airline.

Flying Qatar Airways was yet another of Lucy's long-awaited dreams. She wondered how much better the food would be compared to the leftover *chombo* she ate numerous times before from the Dandora dump.

Once the team boarded the flight, Lucy became visibly excited, unable to sit still or stop talking. Her team members wondered how they were going to put up with her for the long flight. Lucy wished that Chumbana could be with her for the thrill of flying on Qatar. When the flight attendants came around to make sure everybody was seated properly prior to takeoff, Lucy tried to say something to the attendant, but nothing came out. She just smiled, starstruck in meeting someone who was already what she aspired to be.

With the plane starting to taxi toward the runway, the pilot announced to the flight attendants to take their seats.

Lucy felt the plane come to a complete stop. She looked out the window to see what was wrong. Suddenly, there was a loud whirring sound, and her seat began shaking as the plane lurched forward.

The sensation flooded Lucy with panic. Her heart racing, she looked around at the rest of her teammates. They were totally relaxed. Some of them had already fallen asleep. She was not the only one hearing the sounds or enduring the shaking, but from the reaction of others, no one seemed to mind.

The plane picked up more speed, and Lucy glimpsed out the window to the airport, which was moving past the window so fast that it made her dizzy. She closed her eyes and leaned back in her chair.

As Lucy felt herself tilting backward, she opened her eyes again. The ground below her started fading away. The dizziness became vertigo and she was overwhelmed by nausea. She closed her eyes again, hoping it would pass, but it did not.

An uneasiness fell over Lucy and she opened her eyes, desperately digging around for a container to keep from embarrassing herself by getting sick on the plane. She found a paper bag just in time to open it and vomit.

Sylvia asked if she was okay.

"I'm all right." Lucy looked away. She did not think her first flight would be like this. She threw up several more times as the plane continued its climb.

A flight attendant came to check on Lucy when they were able to leave their seats, and she asked Lucy how she was.

Lucy was humiliated by the trouble she had caused. "I have never been on a plane before," she admitted, overcoming her awkward feelings and embarrassment.

"People get sick sometimes; it's nothing to worry about. We are here to make sure you have a comfortable flight," the attendant assured her. "You will feel much better as soon as we get to our cruising altitude."

Lucy gave the attendant a weak smile. "Yes, I'm sure I will feel better. Thank you," she lied, not quite believing what she was saying. Lucy closed her eyes again and prayed that the queasiness would pass. Just in case, she kept the bag gripped tightly in her hand.

The attendant came back again to see how Lucy was doing as the plane reached cruising altitude. Lucy was actually starting to feel a bit better now that the plane had leveled off.

The flight attendant continued checking on Lucy frequently to make sure she was comfortable, and Lucy took the opportunity to ask about working for Qatar Airways and how she became an attendant.

"Qatar Airways is always looking for international cabin crew members," the attendant told her. This made her wonder why the man at Nairobi Aviation College suggested it was a difficult field to get a job in.

Lucy became so engrossed in talking with the flight attendant and watching her tend to passengers that the time passed quickly. She did not even notice when the plane started descending. They landed at Hamad International Airport in Doha, Qatar, where Lucy and her teammates had a three-hour layover before proceeding on to China.

Lucy walked through the terminal in wonder, taking in the beautiful architecture with large pillars and glass skylights, tall and intricate ceilings, and numerous attractions surrounding her. High-end perfume, chocolate, and clothing stores invited her in to browse. She went inside every shop to look around, knowing she could not afford anything. Still, it was fun to experience a world so different than Korogocho. Some of the stores gave away samples of chocolates or perfumes, in which she indulged.

Weaving her way through the shops, she ended up at the center of the terminal, where a gigantic teddy bear display almost as tall as the building itself stared down at her. Many travelers were drawn to it, snapping pictures and selfies. Lucy stood in front of the bear for a full fifteen minutes. Hundreds of passengers brushed past her as she stood looking. She barely noticed that she was surrounded by so many foreign faces.

Lucy walked around by herself without having to fear for her life or getting robbed. It was something she had barely experienced in her life. No matter where she went in Korogocho, she had to be careful.

The sheer size of the terminal made Lucy feel free. She could lose herself in the open space, even with a crowd around her. With so many people crammed into Korogocho, it always felt constrained.

Soon, it was time to board the flight to China. The team flew to Guangzhou, China, and there they transferred again to go to Nanjing where the skating competition was held. Lucy acclimated to flying quickly after the first takeoff. She did not have any more nauseous episodes on the connecting flights. She relaxed now that she knew what to expect.

The team reached Nanjing on the morning of August 28. As they cleared customs and made it to the arrivals area, Lucy tried to talk to a young teenage boy. He was thin and had very pale skin.

She said hello and told him she was in China for a roller-blading competition, and wanted to learn more about China.

The boy started giggling and did not respond. Instead, he pulled out a cell phone and said only a single word. "Picture?"

Lucy did not know what the boy meant. "What is your name?" she asked. The boy giggled again. Then she realized that he did not know English.

"Picture?" he requested again.

Lucy was still confused by what the boy was asking. "You want me to take a picture for you?"

He pointed back and forth between himself and Lucy; then he stood beside her with his phone.

"You want to take a picture with me?" Lucy laughed, flattered. She wondered if he heard about who she was, then smiled as the boy took a picture of them together.

As she looked around at her teammates, she noticed that others were also being asked to take pictures.

Lameck saw her and laughed.

"I guess it's true after all," he said, walking toward her. "Chinese people ask anybody who is different than them to be in pictures. I think they're asking us to take pictures because we're Black and they haven't seen anyone like us before."

She was not sure whether to believe him and asked if he knew where they were supposed to be going.

"The race organizers are going to pick us up and take us to the hotel. Then we will have a few days to settle in and practice. We also need to prepare for the official Roller Games Opening Ceremony on September 2," Lameck answered.

Lucy could not wait to meet the rollerbladers from around the world. She had never interacted with people from different countries or stayed in a fancy hotel before. As much as she tried to focus on something else, the thoughts of doubt that she might make a fool of herself because of her innocence kept creeping back.

Hours passed by as they waited to be picked up and taken to the hotel. Some teammates became irritable as they were already exhausted from the long travels. Lameck tried many times to contact the race organizers but could not get his phone to work. Lucy and her teammates could not get any reception either. Eventually, he gave up and decided it would be easier to just take a bus from the airport to the hotel by themselves.

Lameck coaxed the team to board the shuttle bus from the airport. He did not have the address of the hotel but knew the competition site was somewhere in downtown Nanjing. He assumed that the hotel would have to be close by. If they had any trouble finding it, he was sure they could ask somebody for help.

Lameck's confidence was infectious, but it soon became clear that he had no idea where they were going. He had everyone get off the bus after about forty-five minutes, saying they reached their destination. As the team got off, they found themselves in the middle of a busy road.

"This doesn't feel like the right place," Lucy said.

Lameck insisted it was the right area and proceeded to ask bystanders for more precise directions to where they needed to go. Because of the language barrier, nobody understood what he was saying.

The members of the team tried to talk with anybody who walked by who could understand. A long time passed without any success, and some rollerbladers thought they would have to sleep outside. Several moped along the side of the road, depressed and tired.

Lucy kept approaching every person who came along, certain that one of them would be able to speak English. After trying innumerable times and being asked to take almost as many pictures, Lucy approached a girl who was about her age.

"My name is Lucy. I'm from Kenya, here for a rollerblading competition. My team is lost. Can you help?" she asked.

"What happened?" asked the girl.

Lucy was happy just to get a response in English. "We arrived in Nanjing this morning," she said, "and we are here for a rollerblading competition. We're looking for our hotel. I've been asking everybody if they can help us find it, but I haven't come across anybody who speaks English. We've been here for hours!"

"That sounds terrible," the girl said. "Do you know the name of the hotel?"

Lucy called to Lameck. "This girl speaks English and can help us find our hotel!"

The girl asked Lameck about the competition they were supposed to attend and the hotel name. She had not heard of the competition or the road where it was supposed to be. Lameck admitted he did not know the name of the hotel.

Lucy had one more idea before giving up.

"Do you know any cheap places for us to stay near here?" she asked the girl. "Maybe after we rest, we can try again to find the competition and hotel in the morning."

The girl said she knew an inexpensive place nearby and offered to accompany them there as she was headed in the same direction. They boarded another bus, and in ten minutes, they were in a run-down area. The girl pointed out a small lodge.

"This is the cheapest place I know to stay," she said. The building was like a long warehouse and looked decent from the outside.

Lucy hoped the girl would come inside with them in case they needed help, but she said she had to leave. She assured them that somebody inside would be able to speak English, adding that many foreigners came there.

The team went into the lodge as the girl walked away. Inside, the hotel was not what they expected. Half-naked women walked around the lobby, asking men how much they were willing to pay for their services. The men smoked cigarettes and grabbed the women as they pleased.

While Lameck went to the desk to inquire about the room prices, Lucy tried to stay out of the men's sight. They puffed smoke toward her that was so thick it made it hard for her to breathe without choking.

She was relieved to escape when Lameck called the team together.

"I know this isn't the best accommodation," Lameck said, "but it's starting to get late. We'll stay here for tonight and find the competition tomorrow."

While Lucy should have been happy they found a place to sleep, she felt like crying as she thought about Korogocho. Even though the slum was dangerous, at least it was familiar and she felt at home. The feeling lasted only a minute, giving way to the reason of why they were there. Her aim of becoming the best female rollerblader ever and realizing her dreams of being a flight attendant were more important than where the team slept for one night.

The team had to share rooms to remain within their budget. Lucy volunteered to stay with Sylvia. Inside their room, there was one bed for both of them to sleep on. It was dark and musty, stains covered parts of the thin carpet, and the smell of cigarette and cigar smoke lingered in the air. Lucy did her best to avoid paying attention to the odors as they settled in.

Eager for fresh air, Sylvia asked Lucy if she wanted to go try to find something to eat. Lucy had not eaten all day and was craving some *ugali*. The girls headed out toward the street, wondering where they could find what they craved. As they walked out, two big men by the door leered at the prostitutes in the lobby.

Outside, it was dark and they didn't know anything about where they were.

Lucy had a sudden change of heart. It was difficult to turn down the prospect of food given how hungry she was. But being from Korogocho and knowing what could happen there at night, she was not comfortable taking any risks in a strange place.

"I think we should wait until the morning to eat," she said, surveying the unknown landscape.

The girls returned to their room and tried to get some rest. Lucy heard loud noises from the lobby and growls from her furious stomach. She had a headache from the smell of the smoke but did her best to forget the day's problems until she drifted off into a dark slumber.

The next morning, Lucy woke up feeling like she was going to pass out from weakness. She needed to get something to eat and drink and asked her roommate to go out with her.

They found a small market nearby. Lucy had just 5 yuan (USD 0.75) with her and searched for something she could afford. She was surprised to see that most of the prices were similar to those back home.

Lucy spotted an item in the market that appeared to be a chapati, on sale for only 3 yuan (USD 0.45). It made her mouth water. She unwrapped it and started eating it before they even went up to the counter. Looking around for something to drink, she found a small can of soda that was priced at 2 yuan (USD 0.30), and that was exactly what she needed.

The girls went to the front of the market and stood in line to pay for their food. Lucy had already devoured almost everything by the time she got to the cashier. She handed over 5 yuan for the chapati and soda. The cashier kept her hand outstretched, like she was expecting more money. She glared at Lucy and started berating her.

Lucy's heart jumped into her throat, guessing that she must have misunderstood the prices. She did not have any more money with her.

"I'm really sorry, what's wrong?" she asked.

The cashier did not know English and raised her voice at Lucy, seeming very angry that she wasn't paying her bill.

"Please forgive me," implored Lucy. "It's my first time in China and I don't know how anything works here."

Among the other shoppers waiting in line, one boy understood fragments of English and tried to jump in.

"The cashier is accusing you of stealing food and soda. She says you owe 10 yuan and that if you don't pay, she will call the police," he said to Lucy.

Sylvia tried to step in and offer her own money to pay, but she had only 6 yuan. Lucy begged the woman for forgiveness, explaining that she did not intend to steal anything and offered to wash everything in the market to make up for what she owed. The cashier did not understand, so the boy relayed the offer to her. She shook her head, refusing the proposal.

Lucy explained to the boy that she was from Kenya and how she added up the prices for the food. She didn't have any more money with her, but she wanted to settle her debt. The boy felt sorry for Lucy because he could tell she was not trying to cheat the clerk.

He offered to pay for her, handing the cashier the remaining 10 yuan.

Lucy almost broke into tears thanking the boy for his kindness. She asked how she could pay him back.

"It's not necessary," he said. "Can I just take a picture with both of you?"

The idea that the Chinese people wanted to take pictures with them was already familiar, and Lucy and Sylvia agreed to pose for a picture with him.

When he asked why they were in Nanjing, they explained their story about traveling for the rollerblading competition. He did not know anything about the competition or where it was located. Before parting ways, Sylvia checked with him about the price of her bag of chips as she did not want to make the same mistake as Lucy and infuriate the woman again. She had enough money and purchased it without incident.

The girls walked back toward the hotel eating in silence, flustered by the events at the market. Considering everything that had happened so far, Lucy hoped the trip to China would get better.

A police car driving by them suddenly shot a burst of sirens, flipped on the lights, and pulled toward them. Lucy threw the little that was left of the chapati and soda down on the ground and started running. Sylvia tossed away her chips and followed after her.

The girls ducked behind a tree and held their breath, hoping the police would just go away, but the two officers appeared beside them.

"I'm sorry, please forgive me. I did not mean to cause any trouble," Lucy pled to the officers.

They looked at her and gestured to the girls to follow them to their car. One of the officers opened the door so they could get in.

Lucy asked where they were going, but neither officer answered. Lucy looked at Sylvia, wondering if this was turning into another bad adventure on their trip. When the car stopped a few moments later, the girls were back at the lodge. The place looked like a scene from a movie. Half a dozen police cars surrounded the building, and officers were everywhere. Lucy buried her head in her hands. She could not believe that all this was happening over a mistake she made at the market.

Lucy saw Lameck outside being interrogated by a few policemen. She ran to him, blurting out, "I'm really sorry! I didn't mean to cause any trouble for the team!"

"What did you do?" he asked with a look of bewilderment.

One officer with a shiny badge on his uniform spoke into his phone. The uniform suggested he was the commander of the force. He used a translation app on his phone to communicate with them by translating his speech from Mandarin to English.

The translated message said, "None of you did anything wrong. We are not here to arrest you. We have been searching for you since yesterday. The organizers of the Roller Games informed us that you never arrived." The officer spoke into the phone again and showed Lameck the message. "It is not safe to stay in this lodge. We will take you where you need to go."

As the news spread, members of the team felt relieved and optimistic that their trip might finally get back on track.

The Nanjing police escorted the Kenyan team to the Dingding International Hotel. An intricate gold chandelier welcomed them to the lobby. The hotel building contained a fitness center, a fancy restaurant, and a swimming pool. When Lucy got to her room, she thought someone made a mistake. It was four times the size of her house in Korogocho. She could not believe the entire space was just for her. She dove onto the bed and giggled like a lunatic. The mattress absorbed her body like she landed in a cloud in heaven.

Lucy explored the rest of the room with curiosity. In the bathroom, she turned on the faucet and the steady stream of water surprised her. She could not believe that she could control the temperature. This one room was a whole different world from Korogocho. She could only wonder what else she was missing.

As she continued her investigation, Lameck stopped by her room.

"We have our practice time soon at the track," he said. "Wear your speed suit and bring all your skating equipment with you."

She took a hot shower before pulling on the suit. Then, she went to the hotel restaurant to look at the food that was available. All of it was free for national team members, so she ate until she could not eat anymore.

After eating, she went to the hotel lobby to wait for transportation to the racetrack with her team. Rollerbladers from all around the world gathered there. Lucy saw athletes from South Africa, Senegal, Ivory Coast, Egypt, and other countries she had never heard of.

Each country had their own bus. Lucy was not sure who was paying for everything, but she was not complaining. Her team bus was even nicer than the bus she and Chumbana took to Mombasa. Part of her felt ashamed for reveling in such luxury while people she knew in Korogocho were struggling to survive.

The racetrack was about twenty minutes away from the hotel at the Nanjing Sports Training Center. Seven other teams were already there when the Kenyans arrived. So many countries were competing that the organizers needed to split them all into five groups. Each group was given two training sessions per day to give skaters an opportunity to get acclimated to the environment and speed skating track.

The track was coated with a special blue-colored acrylic resin that was different from the roads Lucy and her teammates were used to skating on in Kenya. It looked like concrete but felt like a smooth rubber. The surface allowed the team to skate faster and grip the ground better on turns.

Lucy observed skaters from other teams during the practices and was sometimes intimidated by their technique, form, and speed. They looked like professionals who had been training their entire lives. She knew it would be tough to compete but focused each session on preparing herself and making the most of her time learning the track.

Day by day, she became increasingly more confident, and by the end of the five-day practice period, she felt ready for her first race.

The World Roller Games finally kicked off on September 2 with an official opening ceremony at the Olympic Sports Center, which was a multipurpose arena in downtown Nanjing. Roads around the arena were shut down by police because there was so much traffic due to the event. Lucy never saw such congestion even in Nairobi before.

The Indian affiliate had so many members that they arrived with four buses. There was one bus just for the team cooks, one bus for administrators, and two buses for the athletes. India was the only team that had traveling cooks because many of the team members were strict vegetarians and they could not find suitable food in China.

Inside the arena, there were more than ten thousand people attending to watch the races. This was the largest crowd Lucy ever saw at a rollerblading event. Before the ceremony began, she met some of the other rollerbladers. The Colombians were very talkative, and she enjoyed their company.

The ceremony started with all the countries being introduced. When Kenya was called, the Kenyan national anthem played over the roar of the thousands of people in the arena. Lucy screamed as loud as she could to cheer her teammates and her country. In that moment, she got chills realizing the incredible opportunity she had to represent Korogocho and all of Kenya. The ceremony was an inspiring way to start the Roller Games World Championships.

The competition spanned the next full week. Lucy participated in a mix of short and long races, all on the same speed skating track where they practiced. Prior to stepping foot on the track, Lucy promised herself that she was going to accomplish something special and return to Korogocho with a medal from the World Games.

Lucy opened up the Roller Games World Championships by competing in the 15,000-meter event. The global stage coupled with the pressure of not wanting to let the team, the Hope Raisers, her community, and her country down weighed on her. She felt more anxious than she was at her first race ever in Kasarani.

As Lucy approached the starting line, she looked around at the hundreds of spectators watching her. She felt numb from nervousness, and her legs were shaking. Lucy had never participated in a 15,000-meter race before and wondered if she had any business trying it for the first time against the world's best skaters.

The girls did their warm-up stretches for the start of the race. They were so focused that they did not even look toward Lucy. The race officials checked in the competitors and assigned them to starting positions. Lucy was not sure how the positions were determined, but she was given a spot at the very back of the lineup. If she wanted to win, she had to work her way up to the front by passing thirty other rollerbladers in the event.

An official told the skaters that this was an elimination race. Those who fell farthest behind the leader got removed from the field over the course of the competition until only the top four rollerbladers remained.

Lucy craned her neck, trying to see who was slotted into the first starting position. The pack was so large that she could not tell who it was. She set a goal of sticking close to the middle of the pack until she had a chance to move up with the leaders.

A second judge responsible for the race start wasted little time after the brief instructions and called out, "Ready! Get set!"

All of a sudden, there was a loud bang from the starting pistol, and the race was underway. The girls ahead of her accelerated rapidly. Lucy did her best to gain some speed but struggled to keep up. These girls were better than anybody she had raced against before.

Although in last place from the beginning, she vowed not to give up and kept propelling herself forward. Meanwhile, the gap between her and the girls in the lead widened. By the time Lucy had finished the first three laps, she was already winded because of the pace. As she entered the fourth lap, she heard a voice over the loudspeaker say, "Skater 3079 eliminated."

Only when Lucy looked at the race number pinned on the front of her suit did she realize she was 3079. She wanted desperately to keep skating and have the chance to catch up, but a race official waved her off the track. She exited, embarrassed to be eliminated so quickly. Her teammates tried to console her, but she could not help but feel that she let Korogocho, Kenya, and the team down.

The next day, Lucy was scheduled for the 10,000-meter race. She thought back to all the times she won the 10,000-meter in Kenya and the attention it brought her in qualifying for the national team. She thought she could bring that same success to the World Roller Games.

The 10,000-meter was also an elimination race, and many of the same girls from the 15,000-meter race were participating. As soon as the starting pistol went off, Lucy put her energy into keeping up with the skaters ahead. A gap opened again, and once more, she found herself left behind. She pushed until her legs burned, but she just could not generate enough speed to stay with the girls.

The pack pulled away until Lucy heard the announcement on the loudspeaker: "Skater 3079 eliminated." She was humiliated that she could not last more than a couple of laps with the other girls in the race despite her best efforts.

She would have one final chance to redeem herself in the 100-meter sprint a few days later. Shorter races were all about acceleration, compared to the 10,000-meter or 15,000-meter race, which required both acceleration and pacing.

As she lined up, she decided on a new strategy. Instead of focusing on the leader or the skaters in front of her, she wanted her attention on the finish line. It would remove the distraction of thinking about other skaters, which could slow her down a few seconds. In the 100-meter, every second mattered.

The race began, and Lucy could feel her new plan was working. She was leading the pack coming out of the first turn. The excitement of being ahead was something she had let distract her. Within 20 meters of the finish, she accidentally put her skate over the line into a competitor's lane.

The race official's voice came over the loudspeaker: "Skater 3079 disqualified."

Lucy berated herself for making a mistake in a race she was leading and could have won. The disappointment stung as much as falling into a boiler at the Dandora dump.

Her teammates tried to comfort her by pointing out that none of them had come close to winning either. To Lucy, her mistake was much more than just some races she lost—it was her future. She needed to pay for her tuition at Nairobi Aviation College and continue supporting the girls across Korogocho, and her silly mistake cost her the last opportunity to win an award.

To forget about their performances, Lameck suggested that the team have some fun in the last few days of the trip. He arranged a dinner at a local restaurant to experience the local culture. The menu was written completely in Mandarin, so nobody could tell from the names what they might be ordering. The team relied on recommendations by the staff.

When the food came to their table, they still did not know what most of it was. Lucy looked around and reached for one of the dishes that looked like chicken. She stuffed her mouth with it and was impressed by the tenderness. She thought it was the best chicken she had ever tasted in her life. It was so good she forgot about her racing woes.

She encouraged her teammates to try the chicken. They passed pieces around the table and agreed that it was really good. She wondered if it was possible to take some back to Korogocho for Chumbana.

One of the English-speaking staff members saw the Kenyans relishing the meat. He came over to their table.

"What do you think of the frog legs? Is this your first time having them?" he asked.

Lucy stared at him with more of her chicken in her hand. "These are frog legs?!"

"Yes!" he said. "It looks like you like them."

Lucy smiled but suddenly wanted to throw up. She felt everything she ate coming back up her throat. Her teammates burst out laughing at their collective naivete. When the reactions subsided, a team member spoke up.

"They're still really good," he said. "I would eat frog legs again!"

The team also visited the best markets, museums, and temples in Nanjing. By the end of two weeks, Lucy was ready to return home. She was grateful for the opportunity to experience a new culture but missed her Hope Raisers teammates, *ugali,* and life in Korogocho. Most importantly, she looked forward to forgetting her performance at the World Championships.

She wondered if everybody in Korogocho already knew of the results. She imagined how disappointed they must have felt. She brooded on the flight back, trying to think of an appropriate apology for letting them down.

When Lucy returned to Korogocho, Daniel, Mutura, and the Hope Raisers were waiting to greet her as she walked into the narrow alley of her home.

"I'm sorry for my performance. I know it wasn't good. I promise I will make you all proud next time," she said.

Daniel laughed and hugged Lucy. "Don't you know you inspired us by just competing against the world's best rollerbladers?"

She was not sure what he meant. Her Hope Raisers teammates chatted excitedly, bombarding her with questions.

"What was it like flying on a plane?" one of her girls asked.

"Was the food good?" said a younger boy.

"How did you like China?" added another girl.

Lucy promised them that she would share everything about her trip at the next Hope Raisers practice.

"How was the chicken?" asked Chumbana.

Lucy joked that she discovered something even better and told her about the frog legs. Chumbana didn't believe Lucy, but she hoped to try frog legs for herself one day.

Jackline and Mama Bonie also stood in the alley.

"I guess I wasn't the best skater in the world," Lucy said, looking at Mama Bonie.

"You're the best skater in the world to everybody here," said Mama Bonie. "Ever since you left for China, all the girls here have been talking about how they want to become like you."

Suddenly, Lucy understood what Daniel had said. The results of her performance at the games were irrelevant. She went and represented Korogocho against the world's best skaters. This proved to the kids around the slum what they could accomplish. If she helped raise the hopes of the children in the slums, that was success in achieving their mission, and that was more than enough for Lucy.

The Hope Raisers Live On

A rollerblading sign on the road that leads to the Korogocho Chief's Camp. This road is reserved for skating practice every day after 2:00 p.m. COURTESY OF NIHAR SUTHAR

As a true story, the lives of the characters and the Hope Raisers do not end with Lucy's ultimate realization upon returning from China.

Lucy went on to compete at many more international skating competitions. In 2018, she won four gold medals at the African Roller Speed Championships in Egypt, cementing her status as one of the best female speed skaters in all of Africa. She remained resolute and put her race earnings toward her flight operations training at Nairobi Aviation College. She is still working hard to complete her studies and achieve her dream of becoming a Qatar Airways flight attendant.

Lucy continues inspiring girls around the slum to fight for their ambitions. More of them are choosing different paths over the limited possibilities of the past. Through Lucy's example, more people believe they can achieve whatever they put their minds to. Many of the girls admired her boldness, tenacity, and perseverance so much that they collaborated with their schools to start rollerblading classes in her honor.

As a result of her impact, Daniel and Mutura appointed Lucy as the official captain and leader of the Hope Raisers skating team. She pushes the kids to practice hard and utilize skating as a discipline to apply to other interests and achieve their goals. Chumbana and a few other children from the Hope Raisers followed in Lucy's footsteps and qualified for the Kenyan national skating team.

Two of their biggest supporters continue to fuel the skaters. Mama Bonie watches the girls skate in Korogocho when she is not busy with her new business of buying and selling vegetables. She gradually lost the ability to do much else because of her thumb injury and declining health. Seeing the girls practice always brings a smile to her face. Jackline still cleans houses in the rich estates bordering Korogocho and brags to the homeowners about her girls' accomplishments. Both Mama Bonie and Jackline could not be prouder of what the Hope Raisers have achieved.

Daniel and Mutura have continued to expand the Hope Raisers to include a range of performing arts, visual arts, education, and sports activities. Their goal remains to uplift as many kids in Korogocho as possible. Even the village chief, who was skeptical of Hope Raisers programs in the past, started backing their initiatives after witnessing Lucy's success and other positive outcomes. He dedicated the entire road in front of his camp near Grogon to skating and declared that every day after 2:00 p.m., no motorbikes, traffic, or other distractions are allowed on the road. This gives children a safe space to practice rollerblading close to home.

At times, the chief still challenges Daniel and Mutura to be sure they maintain their efforts to build a sustainable organization that results in kids getting employed and being lifted out of poverty. Open dialogue like this is what continues to improve the ongoing Hope Raisers initiatives. The interest and successes brought the community together and transformed it from a dismal slum into something special.

For the rest of us, perhaps the greatest lesson to take away from this transformation is that we too are capable of creating change. Oftentimes, we may feel like we are insignificant or that it is impossible to make a real difference. If we take time to understand the problems of people around us and relate to them, we can do our part to make the world a little bit better.

GUIDE TO KOROGOCHO

Background: Korogocho is the fourth-largest slum settlement in Kenya. Land was originally set aside for low-income housing projects. Immigrants who could not be accommodated in the housing arrangements of Nairobi and people evicted from private land or other upper-class settlements were forced into the area.

Location: 11 kilometers (6.8 miles) northeast of Nairobi, the capital of Kenya

Land Area: Approximately 1 to 1.5 square kilometers (.39 to .58 square miles)

Population: 150,000 to 200,000 residents

Ethnicity: Residents of Korogocho come from many different tribes, but the majority are from the Luo and Kikuyu ethnic tribes. There is also a significant Muslim population that migrated from Somalia and parts of northeastern Kenya.

Government: There is little formal government presence in Korogocho. A village chief, similar to a mayor or other elected political official, is appointed as the leader of the community.

Villages: There are nine villages that make up Korogocho:

1. Nyayo: Many lower-class merchants live in this area. They were given the land by President Daniel arap Moi for the purpose of starting the local market, Soko Mjinga.

2. Kisumu Ndogo: The majority of this area's residents are part of the Luo tribe. Kisumu Ndogo is named after Kisumu, Kenya's third-largest city, where inhabitants are also from the Luo tribe.

3. Korogocho A: This was the first settlement area in Korogocho, and is primarily inhabited by members of the Kikuyu tribe.

4. Korogocho B: This is a secondary division of Korogocho A, the first settlement area.

5. Highridge: Highridge is known for its Somali population. Residents migrated from Somalia and parts of northeastern Kenya where Islam was the predominant religion.

6. Grogon A: This area is home to Grogon Road, rumored to be the most dangerous road in Korogocho. It is also the village where most of the gangs that control the Dandora dumpsite are based.

7. Grogon B: This is a secondary division of Grogon A.

8. Gitathuru: This is where the priests from St. John's Community Church live.

9. Ngomongo: Ngomongo is one of the most unstable villages in Korogocho. It is mainly inhabited by people from the Luo ethnic group. They have an intense hatred toward the Kenyan government, as they were evicted from Nairobi by being stoned.

Map of Korogocho:

COURTESY OF PRAJANAPSP

For Book Clubs and Classrooms

THE HOPE RAISERS ARE CHILDREN WHO GREW UP IN THE worst of situations. They did not know a world outside Korogocho existed. None of them had seen rollerblades before. Mutura got involved in a gang and dropped out of school following grade six. Lucy thought women were expected to become prostitutes or get married at a young age.

Then, the Hope Raisers were born. Through art and skating, they fought to transform themselves and their slum. It's a story that will leave you inspired by their strength and dedication. But they don't just want your journey to end there. They want you to go a step further by utilizing the lessons from their experiences to transform your own community.

QUESTIONS FOR DISCUSSION

1. The study conducted by the United Nations Environment Programme outlines the serious health hazards of the Dandora dumpsite on trash pickers and almost two hundred thousand residents of Korogocho. Yet, for thousands of people like Mama Bonie, it can at times be their only source of income and a lifeline for survival. What would you suggest as a solution to this dilemma?

2. What surprised you most about the living conditions in Korogocho? Why?

3. Many community members viewed the Korogocho Slum Upgrading Programme as a failure. If you were given the opportunity to redesign it in hopes of a more successful outcome, how would you do so?

4. In 2013, the Hope Raisers skating team fell apart due to a lack of donations. Some members got fed up and returned to lives of crime and prostitution, causing the village chief to denounce rollerblading. He said the sport was worthless because it did not help kids gain skills, education, or employment. Did you agree with the village chief's assessment at the time? Why?

5. In response to the village chief's disapproval, Daniel and Mutura made changes to the Hope Raisers, the most important of which required members to be enrolled in school if they wanted to rollerblade with the team. If you were in Daniel and Mutura's position, what other adjustments would you have made to ensure that kids were being set up for more sustainable futures through the initiatives?

6. Which character from the Hope Raisers did you relate most closely to and why?

7. What did you find most inspiring about the change the Hope Raisers were able to create in their community, and how do you think you can apply this to your own life and situation?

8. Describe one change you would like to make in your own community. How do you plan on going about doing it?

Help Raise More Hope in Korogocho

If reading about the Hope Raisers has left you searching for a way to connect with them or help further make a difference in Korogocho, they would love to have you join their journey. Today, Hope Raisers initiatives have grown into a range of performing arts, visual arts, education, advocacy awareness, sports, and much more for children and young people in informal settlements. Be part of the movement and help raise more hope at www.thehoperaisers.com.

Notes

Chapter One

1. Njoroge Kimani, *Environmental Pollution and Impacts on Public Health: Implications of the Dandora Municipal Dumping Site in Nairobi, Kenya*, United Nations Environment Programme, accessed November 14, 2021, https://file.ejatlas.org/docs/dandora-landfill-nairobi-kenya/dandorawastedump-reportsummary.pdf.

Chapter Three

1. Andrea Dal Piaz, "Interviews to Hope Raisers Subtitles," April 6, 2009, YouTube video, 7:50, https://youtu.be/XIH91Z0vdZo.

Chapter Four

1. Andrea Dal Piaz, "G8 Song," April 6, 2009, YouTube video, 4:50, https://youtu.be/CQBy4ftNGP8.

Bibliography

"Africa, the G8, and the Blair Initiative." Congressional Research Service. July 20, 2005. http://www.everycrsreport.com/reports /RL32796.html.

Akoth, Steve Ouma, and Raphael Obonyo. "Who Is Korogocho?" In *The Meanings of Social Transformation*, 15–30. Nairobi, Kenya: Pamoja Trust, 2016.

Barczak, Piotr, George Thumbi, and Japheth Oluoch Ogola. "Dandora Landfill in Nairobi, Kenya." Environmental Justice Atlas. April 20, 2015. http://www.ejatlas.org/conflict/dandora-landfill-in -nairobi-kenya.

Chartier, Alexandre. "The Speed Skating Track of the 2016 Worlds in Nanjing." REL. August 25, 2016. https://online-skating.com/the -speed-skating-track-of-the-2016-worlds-in-nanjing.

"Climate, Average Weather of Kenya." ClimaTemps. 2014. http://www .kenya.climatemps.com.

Conrad, David. "The Waste Land." Foreign Policy, FP Group. April 19, 2012. http://www.foreignpolicy.com/2012/04/19/the-waste-land.

Dal Piaz, Andrea. "G8 Song." April 6, 2009. YouTube video, 4:50. https://youtu.be/CQBy4ftNGP8.

———. "Interviews to Hope Raisers Subtitles." April 6, 2009. YouTube video, 7:50. https://youtu.be/XIH91Z0vdZo.

"Feature—Rent Crisis in Nairobi Slums." The New Humanitarian. August 6, 2002. http://www.thenewhumanitarian.org/feature /2002/08/06/feature-rent-crisis-nairobi-slums.

G8 Legal Support Group. "Legal Support Group Statement on the Policing of the G8 Protests." Indymedia UK. July 13, 2005. http://www.indymedia.org.uk/en/2005/07/318170.html.

"Human Rights Watch World Report 1999—Kenya." Refworld, Human Rights Watch. January 1, 1999. http://www.refworld.org /docid/3ae6a8a818.html.

IFRA Nairobi (Institut Français de Recherche en Afrique). "Koro-gocho Slum Upgrading Programme." *East African Review* 44 (2011). May 7, 2019. https://journals.openedition.org/eastafrica /541.

"International Inline Speed Skating Development." World Inline Coach. 2007. http://www.world-inline-coach.com.

Jeffery, Simon, and Matthew Tempest. "200,000 Form Edinburgh Human Chain." *Guardian*, July 2, 2005. http://www.theguardian .com/world/2005/jul/02/g8.uk.

"Kenya Federation of Roller Skating—KFRS." Facebook. 2013. http:// www.facebook.com/www.kfrs.or.ke.

"Kenya Population 2022 (Live)." World Population Review. 2022. http://www.worldpopulationreview.com/countries/kenya -population.

Kimani, Mary. "East Africa Feels Blows of Kenyan Crisis." *Africa Renewal*, April 2008. United Nations. http://www.un.org/africa renewal/magazine/april-2008/east-africa-feels-blows-kenyan -crisis.

Kimani, Njoroge. *Environmental Pollution and Impacts on Public Health: Implications of the Dandora Municipal Dumping Site in Nairobi, Kenya.* United Nations Environment Programme. Accessed November 14, 2021. https://file.ejatlas.org/docs/dandora-land fill-nairobi-kenya/dandorawastedump-reportsummary.pdf.

Lafargue, Jérôme, and Musambayi Katumanga. "Kenya in Turmoil: Post-election Violence and Precarious Pacification." *East African Review* 38 (2008). July 17, 2019. https://journals.openedition.org /eastafrica/665.

Lewis, Simon. *Community Volunteering in Korogocho.* Valuing Volunteering—Kenya. VSO Jitolee and Institute of Development Studies. 2014. https://www.vso.ie/sites/default/files/ic14056_vv _kenya-community_volunteering_in_korogocho-26_08_2015 -low_res.pdf.

"Matatus: Kenya's Decorative Minibuses That Are More Than a Mode of Transport." Agencia EFE. April 17, 2018. http://www.efe.com /efe/english/life/matatus-kenya-s-decorative-minibuses-that-are -more-than-a-mode-of-transport/50000263-3586549.

Mbaria, John. "Kenya: Slum Housing Is Big Business for Nairobi Politicos." Pambazuka News. February 6, 2003. http://www .pambazuka.org/governance/kenya-slum-housing-big-business -nairobi-politicos.

McKinley, James C. "All Sides in Kenya Cry Fraud in Election." *New York Times*, December 31, 1997. http://www.nytimes.com /1997/12/31/world/all-sides-in-kenya-cry-fraud-in-election.html.

"Moi International Sports Complex (MISC), Kasarani." Sports Kenya. 2015. http://www.sportskenya.org/index.php/financing/our -facilities/74-the-moi-international-sports-complex-misc -kasarani.

Muthoni, Millicent. "Kenya-Italy Swap Benefits Korogocho Slums." The Standard. January 14, 2009. http://www.standardmedia.co.ke /home-away/article/1144004020/kenya-italy-swap-benefits -korogocho-slums.

Mutume, Gumisai. "Industrial Countries Write Off Africa's Debt." Africa Renewal, October 2005. United Nations. http://www .un.org/africarenewal/magazine/october-2005/industrial -countries-write-africas-debt.

Mwanza, Kevin. "Efforts to Upgrade Kenya's Slums Undermined by Graft, Lack of Consultation—Researchers." Reuters. February 14, 2018. http://www.reuters.com/article/kenyaNews/idAFL8N1Q 4653.

Shabi, Rachel. "The War on Dissent." *Guardian*, July 2, 2005. http:// www.theguardian.com/politics/2005/jul/02/development.g8.

"Smoking Nairobi Landfill Jeopardizes Schoolchildren's Future." UN Environment Programme. December 21, 2018. https://www.unep .org/news-and-stories/story/smoking-nairobi-landfill-jeopardizes -schoolchildrens-future.

"Youth Organisation: Hope Raisers Initiative." Hope Raisers. Accessed 2019. https://www.hoperaisersinitiative.com/.

Index

Achieng, Lucy, 9; beach visit,
130–33; bullying toward,
71, 75–76, 87, 93, 114;
China trip, 142–150; flight
attendant aspirations of,
106, 133, 137–38, 140–41,
155, 160; Mombasa skating
victory by, 128–29; national
team qualification by,
114–21; new discoveries
by, 140, 142–44, 150–51,
156; nickname of, 94, 115,
138; non-traditional path
of, 9–10, 38–39, 70, 75–76,
81, 88, 93–94, 160; passport
application of, 122–23, 136;
practicing rollerblading by,
70–72, 75–76; role modeling
by, 73, 98–99, 101, 111–12,
117, 133–34, 157–58. *See
also* Roller Games World
Championships

Dandora dumpsite, 2–4;
controlling gangs in, 3;
dangerous conditions of,
2–9, 47; fees for, 3–4

election conflicts, 10–11, 51–52

"G8" song, 43–47
Grogon Road, 14; gang violence
around, 14, 47, 75;
rollerblading on, 66–67,
70–72, 75–76, 99–100,
107–8

Hope Raisers, 40; band
performances of, 45–48, 50,
60; community art-based
organization of, 50–51, 60;
fundraising efforts of, 81–83,
107, 126–27; rollerblading
introduction to, 60–67;
rollerblading success of,
98–99; rollerblading team
formation by, 78–79;
unsustainable programs of,
102–4

Kasarani Skating Championship,
78, 83–95
Kenya Federation of Roller
Skating, 90, 120–21,
139
Korogocho, 12–13; landlord
tensions in, 20–21, 23–28;
living conditions in, 14–15,
30–31, 88

Korogocho Slum Upgrading
Programme, 48, 53, 57;
residents' committee failure
toward, 53–55
Kuria, Mutura, 20, 22, 28, 31–32,
51, 93

Mama Bonie, 4–6; housing
problems of, 20–23, 25–27;
misfortunate life of, 10–12,
24; thumb injury to, 7–10,
16–17, 30–31, 39–40
matatu, 60, 109–11, 127, 131, 139
misunderstanding of local issues,
55–57, 102
Moi Stadium, 89; Hope Raisers
practice at, 108–9; national
team practice at, 120–22
Mombasa Roller Skating
Championship, 126–30

Nairobi skating competition,
109–11
Nyali Beach, 130–34

Omari, Chumbana, 73–75; beach
visit by, 130–33; medical
doctor dreams of, 106,
134; Mombasa skating
victory by, 128–29; Nairobi
skating victory by, 112–13;
rollerblading practices of,
99–101
Onyango, Daniel, 27; musical
interests of, 29, 35–37,
43–45; novel ideas by, 43,
50, 61, 108

Powerslide rollerblades, 90–91,
114, 116, 121

Roller Games World
Championships, 138–39,
143, 153–57; hotel issues
at, 144–47, 150; market
payment commotion at,
147–50; opening ceremony
of, 143, 152–53

Soko Mjinga market, 79–83, 122
St. John's Community Church,
34–35, 38–40, 45, 50–51, 61

trash pickers, 3–6, 15–17

ugali, 29–30, 73–74, 120

About the Author

Nihar Suthar is a writer covering inspirational stories throughout the world. He is the author of *Win No Matter What*, a guide on how to increase your engagement in daily activities, as well as *The Corridor of Uncertainty*, a heartwarming narrative following players from Afghanistan's national cricket team as they attempt to mend their country with peace. Suthar graduated from Cornell University and lives in Tampa, Florida.

9 781538 168738